Dear Fran:

Happy New Year.

Mamie
Jan 1, 1988

Original woodcut of Catherine at
prayer, by Donna J. Surprenant
Madonna House, Combermere

My Heart and I

Interior Conversations
1952-1959

Catherine de Hueck Doherty

ST. BEDE'S PUBLICATIONS
Petersham, Massachusetts

Imprimatur: +Timothy J. Harrington
                 Bishop of Worcester
May 29, 1987

The *Imprimatur* is an official declaration that a book or pamphlet is considered to be free of doctrinal and moral error. It is not implied that those who have granted the *Imprimatur* necessarily agree with the contents, opinions, or statements expressed.

LIBRARY OF CONGRESS CATALOGING-IN-PUBLICATION DATA

Doherty, Catherine de Hueck, 1896-1985
  My heart and I.

  1. Doherty, Catherine de Hueck, 1896-1985—Diaries.
2. Catholics—Biography.   3. Spiritual life—Catholic authors.   I. Title.
BX4705.D56A3   1987   248   87-17287
ISBN 0-932506-59-3

Published by St. Bede's Publications
          P.O. Box 545
          Petersham, MA 01366-0545

To my son, George

Contents

Foreword

Anyone who ever met Catherine Doherty knew that she possessed a spiritual personality with many facets. It can be seen that she, like St. Paul, became all things to all men for the sake of the Gospel. What is it that goes on in the soul of a person that brings them to such a state of spiritual greatness?

Catherine's life during the Friendship House days was notorious for Social Action. She was known as a writer, lecturer, and leader in the laity's awakening of the social issues of the thirties and forties. But by the time she arrived in Combermere in 1947 she appeared to be a broken and defeated woman. Twice she had seen the Apostolate fail. For all intents and purposes she had no reason to begin again.

Little did anyone realize what depths of suffering had gone on in her soul during these active years in the Lay Apostolate. Perhaps the words of her Spiritual Director urging her to pray with greater fervour and to embrace the cross were strengthening words to her. She was told that if we are willing to pay a great price—the willingness to suffer, and suffer a great deal, then a strange power over souls which defies any kind of explanation in which the world can understand, is realized. She had been very generous with Our Lord. She had given her time, her money, and sacrificed physical comfort. But God kept putting these things aside and demanded from her an interior suffering which is infinitely harder than all the external disciplines that she had taken upon herself. She came to realize that this is the only way to restore the world. It was through her pain that she came to know that there are people ready to help the world in easy ways but these ways simply will not endure.

The years with Friendship House had purified and emptied Catherine. Upon her beginning the third phase of her apostolic life in Combermere she entered into the mystical fires of the Holy Trinity. Few in the world realize how truly transformed was this woman by God Himself.

The poems in this volume are human efforts to convey to others the inspired wisdom that was infused in her through the last thirty years of her life. Her prayer grew in depths and union until she no longer lived but Christ Himself lived, spoke and moved through her. Until now Catherine has been known as an outstanding spiritual writer, foundress, and an intellectual. At the heart of Catherine was a mysticism which is given to very few in the Church.

Since poetry has been used through the ages to express intuitions of the supernatural, it was a vehicle that Catherine used frequently. It was one way of her being able to express the emotional, physical, and sense experience that is universal to us all. Its ability to convey human feelings and consciousness stands as a link between the natural and the supernatural.

Many of these poems refer to Father John Callahan. He arrived in Combermere in 1952 and received an extraordinary grace which literally transformed his vocation as diocesan priest to that of becoming the founder priest of the Madonna House Apostolate. Subsequently fifteen Madonna House priests and eight-two Associate priests followed in this vocation and, undoubtedly, we are only seeing the beginning of a new order of men, women and priests entering into the life of the Church in the twentieth century. Father Callahan was also given the privilege of being Catherine's spiritual director from 1952 until his death April 7, 1974. In her person he was a most remarkable priest. He was highly skilled in leading souls on the path to sanctity. He will undoubtedly be better known in years to come. Much of what has been hidden will slowly be revealed of the inner life of both of these giants of the faith.

The Church has lived through many upheavals. No one can deny that the Church today is facing one of the greatest, if not the greatest, crisis of its two thousand years of history. Into that turbulence has come a profound trial of the priesthood. But God never abandons His Church. Catherine de Hueck Doherty was formed in the heart of God through the Russian Revolution, the First World War, Second World War, and through the cracking of all of western civilization. She foresaw years ago that the difficulties of the era in which we live had at their heart a spiritual confrontation of immense magnitude. Her intellectual genius was purified until the very breath of the Trinity and Our Lady taught her all that she has given to the Church. But her deepest vocation was to lay her life down for the priests of the Church today. She loved priests with a passion because they give us God. She suffered, atoned, prayed, and lived, that the priesthood would be restored so that the Church could be restored.

Father John Callahan was a hidden but very important instrument in this vocation of Catherine's. The poems in this volume give us a reflection of the journey that they shared during their years shaping the present family of Madonna House. It was a journey that began in the heart of God and has slowly moved, creating a tapestry of love that can be seen in every facet of daily life.

Jean Fox
Madonna House
Combermere, Ontario

Today my heart and I are poised for the start of a new journey that seems to be contained within the journey inward we have been on since long before we can remember.

This journey within a journey is strange to us. As yet we do not know, my heart and I, where we will go. For as yet we do not seem to know how we can go outward and inward at the same time. But that is what we are poised for, my heart and I.

One thing we know: we shall walk in company of the holy Three—his loneliness, his pain, his tears. For this our second journey, it seems, will take us into the souls of men. It will not only follow his footsteps there; it will make us enter in.

We do not know as yet, my heart and I, why we are afraid of staying in the hearts of men. But that we do know: fear encompasses us and won't as yet let go of us. Yet they will, when time is nigh to start. For we have, my heart and I, his power to command the things of hell when we go or do his holy will's desire.

Today at Mass a strange pain and light touched us. Quite suddenly it was as if we could read the hearts of men. They seemed a book with clear, sharp print that we could read from far away. We were disturbed, my heart and I, until he came and laid our fears away.

Yes, we are poised, my heart and I, for a new journey. As yet we do not know where we will go, except that it will take us into the souls, the hearts of men.

And we have to stand very still for yet a time, a while, because he who has our soul in his anointed hands must furnish us with all our needs, teach us all the ways we shall go, and what and how to do on the way.

There is in us today a strange lightness. And it seems as if we truly are contained within the very inner chamber of God's heart. And now we are as if truly set apart, our face turned toward his face.

He is indeed the most beautiful of men and our gaze is
riveted on his. We seem to vanish, my heart and I, and yet
we know it is not so.

The weight of time gets heavier. But we are glad to do
what is his desire. It seems that is all we live for.

Pearl of Great Price   *January 14, 1952*

Translucent, shimmering, radiant, iridescent, catching
all shades of light and then reflecting them anew, with
beauty unsurpassed, unknown, incomprehensible, unfathomable, beyond all sense, all touch, the pearl of great
price hung there immense, betwixt and between, before
my eyes.

And yet, my heart and I, without seeing, had known so
long, so very long ago, that it was there. And knowing
without seeing, had sold all that we possessed and then
thrown ourselves into the bargain; then arisen and gone
in search of it, in a strange economy of motion that did
not count time as men do count, but followed the footsteps of him who parcelled time for us on earth and took
into consideration rain, sun, cold, heat, dark of night. But
we just went on and on in search, through blinding pain,
through blood, through loneliness that seared our very
lives away. Yes, went on in search of that translucent,
shimmering, radiant, iridescent pearl of great price that
hung in beauty unsurpassed betwixt and between now,
before our very own eyes.

And yet, behold, my heart and I know suddenly sadness beyond all knowing. It encompasses us beyond all
power, it seems, of bearing it. And yet we bear it. The
pearl grows, it lives, it moves; and there before our blur-
ring eyes, it changes shape. And then from nowhere another hangs beside it, a little higher, as beautiful as the
one beyond all price of having.

The sadness grows where joy should reign, and eyes that should be all enthralled barely can see the beauty uncreated that lies within the ever growing, changing pearls that seem to slowly come closer to us.

My heart and I have lost our sight. We are as if we were sightless, blind, lost in a darkness of loneliness, of pain, of shed and unshed tears. All streaming, flowing, converging into us from strange and hidden corners of the earth, its cities and its wilderness, they enter us, they fill us to the brim. Behold, one more drop of this and they will drown us. And then we shall not be ourselves, my heart and I, but just the woes, the pain, the loneliness, the tears shed and unshed of all from everywhere who walk the earth alone, misunderstood, forgotten, poor, and grovel in the dust of other men's hardness of heart.

But no, this is not so. We are within the pearl beyond all price. And now we, they, or it, are the tears of Christ.

Oh, what is inside the priceless pearl, and how did I and my foolish, sluggish heart get in, and why?

"You are within my tears, child of my heart, because you let me weep them on your breasts that, as you know, taste better to me than wine."

I, Lord of my heart, let you weep upon my breasts—when, how, I do not know.

"Rest, child, and see how many wept when you were but fifteen, my Mother's age. Remember blood, remember war, remember darkness, fear, despair. How many wept themselves back into faith upon your breasts?

"And then remember when you were poor, as I was poor. Your manger they called 'displaced persons' or 'refugees.' You were yourself so full of tears, but you did not seek a place to weep. You let your breasts absorb the tears of countless others. Remember them.

"And then when you went through my hidden years, buffeted from door to door, hungry and cold and all alone; do you remember them, the kids that were so young and so alone, even as you? Remember how so

many came and wept against your naked breasts in rooms
so cold that your breath froze and so did theirs. Remember that?

"And then you took me at my word and sold all things
that seemed to belong to you. And throwing yourself into
the bargain, you descended into my ascending. And from
that day, how many came to weep on your warm breasts
to rest and to drink the wine from them—remember that?

"You did not know, you could not know that it was I
that changed their tears into a wine that was so fine, so
perfect, that those who drank of it got truly drunk the
way men should on love of me.

"Oh lovely child of my great love, oh foolish heart that
was so wise and walked so gallantly, so simply, in utter
faith. You did not know, you did not guess that it was
always I who wept upon your breasts.

"But now you know. For a while I took you in, into my
tears shed for the love of all mankind so often and so
bitterly.

"Because your breasts are filled with tears that healed
and brought my love to men as soon as they touched
them, I, the Lord your God, give you tonight the gift of
tears, to weep when I shall command. And as you weep,
these tears will bring the souls of men into my heart."

Domain Of Lady Pain   *March 6, 1952*

The domain of Lady Pain is infinite. My heart and I
begin to know a little bit the extent of it. But now we
know that we will dwell unto the end in some part of it.

Love touched us lightly with his lips the other day and
begged us to take a grain of his infinite pain away from
him; because those who love share each other's burdens,
so he said.

My heart and I just smiled and said we are so very
small in size of soul; but our love is big because he made

it so. And may we please be beggars too and beg to share, not a grain of his pain, but all of it. For we felt sure his grace would help us to do so and our love for him would help his grace—for both were one.

Strange as this seems, his tear-stained face became like the sun and he smiled at us; and bending down, with tender hands he laid his pain, his cross, on us.

That is how we learned to see the extent of the domain of Lady Pain. That is how we now know we shall dwell in some part of it unto the end of our days.

There is in us today a sea of pain, because our Beloved loves so well he always takes upon himself more pain to win the soul of man, his bride, back to himself; or to protect his very own, his priests; or to assist the man in white who is the incarnation of his might to us on earth.

That is how we dwell in pain, my heart and I.

Yet there is deep stillness in us. We enter now into the solitude of it. The deep unbroken silence of love in pain encompasses my heart and me.

Today we know that yesterday he cut us off from all that is not himself and the affairs of Father, Son, and Holy Spirit. Today we know that we are indeed to enter the deep darkness of faith. This is the day, this is the time. For this we lived, for this we die.

Last night he gave us a golden key flecked with red, blood red, that is. And then he said, "I am the lock. You must use the key whenever I call, and then without a backward glance enter the darkness of faith in the solitude and silence of love and pain.

"Woman of the strange land my Mother loves, and so do I, the time has come for you to enter into my passion and the dark I knew. You have completed the novitiate of love's first school. You have loved well according to the way and lights I gave. But now you enter into the way, and when you next will see the light, it will be because you see my face with your own eyes.

"You will have much given to you along this way, at my

good time and pleasure too. But now you walk the ways of night, naked and with a thousand winds like swords piercing your heart. Before you stretches out in all its immensity the domain of Lady Pain that I dwelled in for many days. My hours to you are years, my dear. From now on don't call yourself so small, for you have grown up and shall drink of my cup."

Christ Was Nigh   *September 30, 1952*

The Lord called me suddenly out of the marketplace where I was busy about his Father's business. Yes, the Lord called me suddenly out of the marketplace and the heat of the day. He called me suddenly, into his shade, and then into his glory.

But I did not arise and go as I should have done at once when the Lord spoke. For I looked at my garments and saw them as they were—soiled and in tatters from the sweat and the labors of the marketplace, from the heat of the day and the labor of the night.

No, I did not arise and go at once, for I saw more. I saw my soul covered with the leprosy of sins, many sins, sins forgiven and shriven. I saw my soul still covered with scars, the white, shining scars that the leprosy of sin leaves behind always.

No, I did not arise and go as I should have, in answer to the call of the Lord! I held back for an instant called time. Held back because I saw myself as my Lord's Father sees me, and I was sorely afraid!

But my Lord bent down, down, to the thing of ugliness, sweat and scars that was I. Yes, the Lord bent down, down, and lifting my face into his cupped hands, kissed me with the kiss of his mouth.

And I became as white as the new fallen snow, and all my scars vanished beneath the touch of his lips. And my youth was renewed, and beauty shone forth from me. For

I became clothed with the kiss of his mouth. Then I arose from the depths of the marketplace, and I left the heat of the day behind me. I became a garden enclosed in a walled city. And the Lord shut the door of the garden that is I and took the keys away.

Now I am all his, a garden enclosed where he takes delight whenever he wishes. For now he is my beloved, a seal upon my heart; and my mouth forever knows the kiss of his mouth, and my breasts the touch of his hand.

I am his garden! I lie in the sun of his passion, or in the night of his love, always. Now the will of my Lord is mine, and I have no other!

My Lord And I Bedecked With Love *October 1, 1952*

Today the Lord took me by the hand and led me unto a high mountain. And we stood there, my Lord and I, hand in hand for a long time in the all-entrancing silence of his love and my desire.

Then my Lord spoke, and his voice was the soul of all music. I knew then that the great music of all generations that were and were to come was but a feeble echo of my Lord's voice.

As I listened to my Lord's voice, my heart melted away in utter love, and I was as if I were not. For the voice of my Lord had entered into me; had entered into me like the tongue of a lover enters the mouth of the beloved and draws her into himself, to be lost in him who is love.

Slowly, from far away, the words of my Lord came again to me and he said:

"I open my treasure chest for the souls I love and I bedeck them with the beauty that lies therein, hidden from the eyes of those who do not love me alone.

"Yes, at the feet of the souls who love me utterly, passionately, I lay the hidden treasures of my own creation.

"Behold then, beloved of my heart, the treasures I give

you this day. Here are wild asters whose blue will match and enhance the blue of your eyes. I created them both. Both are mine. From all eternity I knew I would bring them together for my delight.

"I myself am the seal on your heart. From all others I will hide my seal. I will cover it with the red and gold of the autumn leaves and I will fashion them into a bodice of unsurpassing beauty, blending the colors with my blood, my precious blood that I shed for you so passionately on Golgotha.

"No one will know that the seal on your heart is I; for the red of the leaves will cover, will hide the blood of my heart that made the seal on yours."

The words of my Lord grew faint in my ears. And again I was as if I were not. For I could not find myself in the voice of my Lord that was like a kiss drawing me out of myself and into the fire of his holy silence in which his love spoke without words.

My Lord led me out of the great silence and again I heard his words and he said:

"Green is the color in which I bedecked the earth. Green is the color of hope. We shall fashion garments to cover your limbs with the emeralds of the earth.

"Light blue asters for your hair, red leaves for your breasts, and soft greens for your limbs. Sapphires, rubies, emeralds for my beloved."

And as my Lord spoke, he clothed my nakedness in the precious stones of his creation. And I stood before my Lord bedecked as he wished me to be, fainting with love.

The Living God   *October 20, 1952*

I saw the Father of my Lord as in a glass, darkly, and knew another love pour into my heart. A love that made me strong. For God the Father is a Mother too. Paternity and maternity do not co-exist one without the other.

My Lord gave me fecundity; his Father blessed it in maternity. Then the Wind, the Flame, the Dove with the wings of blazing red (the color of my Lover's Blood, and of love—the love of God the Father for the Son) appeared, and touched me with his wings of red. And I became a flame so bright that where I walk now there is no night.

He is the Wind, the mighty Breath of God, that bends and sways the reed, the wheat, the waves. A blade of grass he will not break, but mighty oaks he splinters with a touch and leaves the ground bare, scattered with wooden bits.

He hates pride. He is the Wind. He took me up, and now I live a life betwixt and between. Like a feather I float on the endless currents of his might; and yet I live earthbound too, because my Lover wants me to.

Behold the daughter of the King, and of his Son. Behold the wife, fecund in him and in his King's maternity, who rests on her Lover's breast and floats with the Wind that *is* the love of Father and of Son. A blazing Dove, the color of his Blood. All this happened in a church that wasn't really a church at all, but just a little hall.

Yet, there I knew the Three that are One, and held Them to my breast where my Lover rests, and where rests the Father, his Son, and their Love, the blazing Dove.

I went out of myself and cried as men are wont to cry when they fall into the hands of the living God. Yet, my cry held other things than pain which is Love's domain. It held delight, and joy, and utter, complete surrender. And words fled me like frightened birds; but silence found voice in song.

And lying there, prostrate at my Lover's feet, I sang without words. But oh, so loud my puny hymn of love:

"Behold the handmaid of the Lord who is all thine, thy slave, thy chattel, thy queen, thy maid. Behold, my Lord, and know that I am not, for I am dissolved in you. And yet I am a woman, yet a thing call me. And ere thy call has died in music surpassing fair, I shall be there. For I forever wait at thy gates. Throw me away into the darkness of the night. I shall lie still, just where I fall, and wait for thee to come and pick me up.

"Behold thy handmaid, oh my Lord. My back is straight and waits for any yoke thy love may wish to place upon it. I know I shall go on with thy grace whichever way you send me with thy load. If it is pain, I know my love will grow and make it light because it is thine. If joy, I'll bend a little. For joys are heavier than your pain for me a mortal. For I can match my steps to yours when laden with a cross. You walk so slowly. But I can't run like a bridegroom from the chamber of his bride unless you teach me how.

"Behold thy handmaid, oh my Lord, who is all thine. I am obedience. A glance, a word, a wish, and I run, because I must, because I wish, because I love to be all thine. Oh, Lover of my soul, my Lord, my God, make what thou wilt of me from now until eternity. For there is not a thought, a hair, a spot in me that is not thine."

Then silence lost its song, and I was back, prostrate at my Lover's feet, all spent, and yet burning with a flame so bright that where I walk there is no night.

Now I know that it is so—that human tongue cannot explain, nor try to tell, what the soul has seen, and held, and touched. To one alone can it be said, to a priest of God who knows the language of love, in stuttering words. He alone has the powers of my Lord to still the soul's raging sea, its mortal terror, its holy awe, protect it from the foe, and from itself, and lead it into the roads of pain and joy, adjust God's yoke with hands anointed for the task.

For God has placed him in His stead, to measure for the soul the span of betwixt and between, and how to live therein; to keep it floating on the endless currents of His might, and to adorn it for His delight. That is the power of His priest, for he too can take an old and ugly thing—a soul in sin—and make it into a garden enclosed, of beauty unsurpassed, undreamed of by men, where God will come and rest.

But gardener, beware! There is no other task for thee but this (He speaks to thee). You cannot fall asleep. For then the foe will come and make thy newly sown garden dead again. Nor can you take your eyes off your Beloved. Because a soul is young, untutored, and afraid of love. You must teach her how to love. And for this *you* must love more and more, for your soul (the one entrusted to you) is His before He bends to make her His own. Nor will He touch the souls of others but through your anointed hands—unless you fail Him. And then the gates of hell will open wide for you!

He wants you poor in goods of earth, because He needs the space to fill with treasures of His grace. For you are the cellar where He keeps His choicest wine, His whitest bread, to feed all hungers and quench all thirsts.

He wants you poor because you are His feet, His hands, His eyes. Through you He seeks the lost and wandering sheep. How can your feet be fleet when you are burdened so with love of earthly goods.

And so, oh priest that is another Christ, arise, and give thyself to God the Son as He gave Himself to His Father. Be naked, poor, a flame. For the Dove breathes with thy breath, the Son loves with thy love and feeds His loves through thee. Then God the Father comes and gives thee his paternity so that you too beget the brides his Son died for with mad desire.

Yes, all this happened in a church that wasn't really a church at all, but just a little hall. And yet, it was the House of God, *terribilis*, and holy ground, for He dwelt there, my Love, my God, and All.

A Rendezvous   *October 20, 1952*

The night enveloped me into its warm, quiet darkness; I went in depth, a feather slowly falling into the womb of timelessness. I had a rendezvous to keep with Love. The place? Where time surrenders to eternity. The hour? Where hours cease to be.

I had a rendezvous to keep with Love—I did. And my Beloved called me into his tent; his breath, fragrant with the fragrance of a million springs, and all beatitude was upon me.

My soul—white, virginal, and pure—stood naked by his couch and unafraid. His breath came like a wind and made me grow until on tiptoes I stood and felt the angels comb my hair.

And then my Lord and God arose, and Beauty uncreated caught my human breath and made me faint with love. But I stood straight and unafraid, for I was his and he was mine from all eternity.

He drew me nigh, his mouth met mine. And then I knew fecundity in God was mine. And my soul saw the children of my Lord and mine—souls, souls, and more souls than human eyes could count. And then the night closed in. I knew no more till next I heard the voice of my Lord and Love:

"Into the soul I choose to make my spouse I bring my Father and my Love for him and his for Me, and We take up our abode in thee. Behold my face and see my Father's there. For only thus can you behold his majesty and live. And yet you have, for you see Me!

"And whom I love is his. I paid the price, so I can bring my love before his face. For he is I and I am he. And I shall come myself, alone. When? You know not."

I had a rendezvous to keep, where time meets timelessness and space is not. The tent is gone, so is my Lord, but I am his and his fecundity is mine, for souls.

I am immense in him. My toes stand on the earth and angels comb my hair. Don't come too near, you, to jeer or hurt or desecrate what he had made his own. For I in him am clothed with his might. Beware, for his is vengeance and he will repay.

I had a rendezvous to keep last night. And so I did!

My Heart Is Full Of Fears   *October 23, 1952*

My heart and I are full of fears tonight. Why?
I am the one who saw my Lover's Father's face. And it was I the Dove touched with the tip of its flaming crimson wing. Why then am I afraid tonight? For where I walk, there is no night.
And yet my heart and I are full of fears tonight. Why?
Is it a fear that *he* will stop our journey to the land of ecstasy and pain? But who can stand betwixt my Love and me, oh frightened heart?
Don't beat so fast. The way is long, the night so dark. You need your strength, and I, the flaming light of courage and of faith. Why?
Oh, it is you, my Love, my God, my All, who speak to me in accents pitiful and low. Stand still, my frightened heart, lest I should lose a breath, a sight of my Lord's whisper.
The desert, the desert, the desert.
What desert? Yours? But he knew you not. You did not know him and yet allowed the tempter to tempt the majesty of God.
Stand still, my fearful heart. Stand still. Don't run. This is the test. Stand still, or I will tear you out and be without a fearful heart. Between the sharing of your pain by us, my heart and me, you say there stands the desert that we must traverse tonight, my heart and I.
For those who love man and God must walk the road you walked on earth. And you did stay the forty days to fast and pray, so as to meet Satan in all his pomp and pride and glory, the fool who thought he could tempt God.
But then he was not sure. He did not know that you were he, infinity and majesty, Creator blessed and holy was your name. And yet he spoke thrice; thrice you answered him.
But you are you and I am I. Oh Lord my God, behold

my frightened heart and I lie in the bitter dust of fear.
Your silence is complete. Why don't you speak, my Love,
my Lord, to me?

You wait, you wait on me, my frightened heart. And I,
to shake the bitter dust of fear, run and run into the desert
dark to share with you. What? What? Have I the words of
life? Have I the might the Son of Man and God showed
that night so long ago?

For whom? For what? And why must I and my frightened heart go where you went alone and unafraid?

Does love question? Does it ask for whom or what or
why? Love runs. Love leaps. Love keeps its tryst no matter if it dies or lives. Oh frightened heart, throw out all
fears, for you and I will go, will run, will leap where my
Love, my God, sends us tonight.

And if we have to face the darkness of Satan's might,
we will, in him who strengthens all he touches and beholds close to his heart. Afraid or not, my Lord, I will
your will. Into your desert I shall go tonight and stay until
you wish, obedient to your holy will.

My heart and I will go in utter silence, for this is utter
faith that questions not, but enters hell because of love.
And so, oh frightened heart, throw off your fears and
walk alone wherever he wishes you to go tonight. And
ask not why.

For beyond the rim of hell that has to be traversed for
love, lies ecstasy. And no one can touch its rim unless it
be through him, oh frightened heart that must throw off
its fears.

And so arise and let us go, for love, for God, for souls.
Come on, my heart. There is no time to lose tonight. Tonight we fight, my heart and I, for his domain. And we
extend the fight into the land of Satan, because my God,
my Love, desires it so. That we go beyond, we must not
ask, we must not know.

Come on, my heart. Arise. There is no time to lose

tonight, for it is dark, with a dark darkness; in many souls he reigns.

Come on, my heart. There is no time to lose tonight.

Rubies   *October 23, 1952*

I stood before my Lord, bedecked as he wished me to be, in emeralds, sapphires, fainting with love. And the voice of my Lord whispered into my soul from afar:

"Rubies, to hide the seal of my precious Blood on your heart. Rubies, to hide the slow, penetrating of my Blood into thy heart and through thy heart into the whole that is thee. So that I and my Blood live in thee and thou livest not—livest not, yet livest. To make thee ready for the slow martyrdom of love that now has already begun in thee. To make thee ready for the unquenchable hunger and the devouring flame that will last until the moment (which thou knowest not) when I shall send my beautiful messenger, the angel of death, to call thee forever to me, thy Bridegroom!

"I made myself the seal on thy heart with my precious Blood. I made it so that you shine with the flame that henceforth will consume *thee*! And set others on fire with love of Me! I gave thee the unquenchable, insatiable hunger for *Me* and *my* love, so that, driven by it, you will arise and search for Me. And searching, carry the flame I lit within you everywhere, lighting the darkness for the feet of souls, many souls.

"This is why thy breasts are bedecked with rubies, beloved!

"Emeralds are the color of hope, of the green and eternal renewal of the earth. Hope that will walk with thee, help thee in thy search for me when, in order to bring light to others through thee, I will hide myself from thee. Hide myself from thee so you can arise and search for me, shedding the light of thy burning love for me that comes from the seal I placed on thy heart, the seal that is *I!*

"Yes, hope will walk with thee in the endless path of the dark nights, when, unable to rest, you will arise in search of *Me!* Hope will be also the coin of my love which you will give to those poised on the brink of despair. Hope will be in your hand like a bird in a nest, to let fly wherever you wish it to go. But like a homing pigeon, it will come back to thee. It will come back to thy hand, beloved, to be sent out again and again.

"Sapphires—the blues that blend into whites to fashion my Mother's glory. Softly I lay them on thy head to give thee the blessing of her love, her silence, her wisdom, her humility. I give them to make them a channel for my graces which all must pass through her hands. Graces that will prepare thee for the death I wish for thee. The death of martyrdom in which my precious Blood will mingle with thy human blood and sow the seeds of glory to come in days not yet born, in souls not yet sent to the exile of the earth.

"Rubies, emeralds, sapphires to bedeck thy nakedness, to fashion thee into an instrument of my love."

I stood before my Lord, bedecked as he wished me to be. And my will was that of my Lord. I had no other!

My Foolish Heart At Rest   *October 26, 1952*
Feast of Christ the King

My foolish heart at rest with thee. It lies so utterly small and still within thy hand. My foolish heart and I came here to pray. And you put us to sleep within your heart. A strange and holy sleep we sleep, my heart and I within your heart.

For who can tell where sleep meets dawn? And rest night? And whence both arise? The road is dark. The road is long. Sleep foolish heart. Rest while you can!

"This is my day, and I am King, and you so small, so strange, so shy, so young in all my ways of love. You are my queen, my slave, my love. I know your thoughts. And you are right: nothingness is my delight. For I can fashion everything from its shining translucency. Remain thou such, and you will someday be with me in ecstasy.

"Sleep foolish heart. Rest while you can, strange child from my Mother's land. She loves it so, and so do I. Behold, it dies with me again and again only to be refined into a sword, into a flame that will bring my kingdom back to me.

"Sleep foolish heart. Rest while you can, strange child from my Mother's land. She dwells there now. Rest while you can. For you shall be lifted up with me and die a thousand deaths for me.

"Did you not know this? This is my day, I am a King, and you my queen. Behold my throne, a plank of wood, another one. The two shaped in a cross that stands alone against a threatening sky. A strange and awesome throne for but *one* King!

"Rest foolish heart, sleep while you can, strange child from a distant land. The time is nigh. They'll wake you up and drag you through a night that will lay wrapt with hate and lust. Naked, alone unto my throne, each step steeped in my blood.

"And then, to mocking and jeers they will nail you too unto my throne, my queen. And you will die against my breast for love of me. Strange woman from a far and distant land my Mother brought to me to see thy burning heart. I found it fair. And now, because of that, you are my own, here on my cross, my throne, with me alone, oh foolish heart!

"Rest while you can, sleep while you may. For soon it shall be noon and time to eat the meat of saints. For there is much for you to do before you die! I thirst, I thirst for

souls alone! Arise, go! Bring me to drink. Sitio, I thirst.
You know where to go. He will show the way. Obey, and
bring me souls!!

"He is the sword and you the flame. You stand alone
with me while he makes straight my paths for thee. His
face must look into my Father's face and see there Love
that sends a Son to save the world. Let him send thee
likewise into the darkness of all pain, into the night, to
end on my cross alone with me, while he prepares all
paths to me for thee.

"Let him prepare thee now for the days to come. He is
your guide into my kingdom. For this I laid him low and
raised him up again, that he should take my pain, my
loneliness, and know my throne before he lays you there.

"Rest, child from the strange land my Mother loves.
Sleep while you can."

Where Shall We Go?   *October 27, 1952*

Behold red. A color? Or a flame? So many things are
red and all alive. Why?

My heart and I are full of fears tonight. We crouch. We
hide. From what? Why?

Where shall we go, my heart and I? Where can we hide
our mortal fear that comes from where? Why?

My heart and I seek a dark place, but there is none
anywhere. Why? We want to run, my heart and I, away
from wind, from sky. Where? Why?

It is the red that frightens us tonight, my heart and me.
Why? Red—a color or a flame?

"Oh, foolish heart, stand still and know. There is no
darkness dark enough where I can't go and bring the red
of my burning heart to you and light it up. Red is the
color of my blood. Red is a flame. You know why.

"Oh, foolish heart, where can you go away from red,
away from me? Oh foolish heart, you are afraid because

you know that red becomes you so, and that some day I shall bedeck you in the flaming colors of ecstasy.

"Where love, my love, and pain, my pain, keep rendezvous again, again, in martyr's blood that flows so red and lights a flame in hearts of men that never dies.

"Stand still, oh foolish heart, and know that red becomes you so; and that some day I will bedeck you in the bright red of martyrdom and ecstasy."

O, Foolish Heart   *November 1, 1952*

"Oh, foolish heart. I lift thee up because you are so full of fears. You stand so still when you must run away from fears into my arms.

"Oh, foolish heart. I bend so low to reach thee. Lying there on roads long turned to dust and overgrown with weeds. Leave fears behind and run, run into my heart.

"Oh, foolish heart. I walk so slowly to match my giant stride to thine. Behold me, the One who leaps, the One who runs from sun to sun, from star to star, walking so slowly. All for a foolish heart all filled with fears, begotten from too many tears.

"Oh, come beloved. Shed all your fears and love Me *now*, without tears, and know that perfect love casts out *all fears*.

"Oh, foolish heart. I stand so still and wait, and wait before thy door, so barred, so closed with a thousand locks of fear. I made the door, and you are the locks. I can't come in until you take your love and smash the locks and call Me in.

"Oh, foolish heart. What thoughts are these? I am the Lord, thy God, and I can choose whom I desire. And I can leave and I can take whatever I can make. And that is all. Be silent, be still, and hear my voice. Deny me not, thy living God. The broken I make whole, without a touch. The sick are healed by a word or glance, as it pleases me. The dead arise when I command. The living die when I desire. I am thy living God. Remember this. If I choose thee, don't ask me why. For you are mine before you are. If I desire to touch the mire that mirrors its fears into your eyes, then know that you become clean as snow because I wish it so, and your eyes henceforth mirror skies.

"Oh, foolish heart. Arise and come into the heart of love that is thy God. Know perfect love. Forget all fears, for I want souls through you, my love. You are a bed and I the River that slackens all that drink from it. Be still, be fair, be clean, be ready to turn, to bend at my desire.

"You are a pipe and I the Piper. I call the tune in the dark night, and in the light of day. And all I ask is that you lie still, close to my head; don't go away. Today I want you still to fight for souls wherever I will. Tomorrow you will be wax for my fire.

"What will come after is not for you to know until I want it so. All I demand is pure obedience to my command, for I, Beloved, I am thy living God."

Be Not Afraid   *November 2, 1952*

"Be not afraid, dear heart, it is I. I know my weight is all eternity, but I will make it light, like thistledown sown in the night.

"Be not afraid, dear heart, it is I. I know the awesomeness that is I, the Uncreated, but I shall hide its blinding light in the quiet of the thousand nights that are so still.

"Be not afraid, dear heart, it is I. I know my might, but I shall hide it in the wind and gently sing a child to sleep before she is my bride.

"Stand straight, dear heart, be not afraid. It is I. And you with hair of many hues. A child at heart who did not know that God loved her so.

"Behold I made thee fair and send thee into a world of woe, alone. I let thee know the weight of tears, the shed and the unshed, the shriven and the dead.

"I let thee go alone and face the terrors of the dark that dwell in hearts that have forgotten me. I stood you on a mountain top and bade you start your descent in the dark, your journey inward that leads to Me—and ecstasy.

"You were so small, so young, and so alone, without a throne. Into the valley of a thousand shadows you went obediently according to my word. And then you descended again into the pits of hell that dwell (as does my kingdom) on the earth that should be fair like your hair.

"I send you there myself, thy God, for this is the very road I trod alone. And now you had to slowly retrace my steps. For at the end was I, thy living God.

"You went and fell so many times, for it was bleak, and it was dark, and you were all alone, or so you thought. You went according to my word. The stones were sharp, the wind was cold. Your blood was red upon the stones. But mine was redder still, and you went on.

"Once or twice you lost your way. I sent an angel in the wind to get you back into the dark, onto the stones that cut; and you went on alone. I bent and touched you who were so small. And lo! The dark grew darker, and you sweated blood. For there you were, without kith or kin. I touched and took all that I once gave to you.

"You were so small and all alone. My queen without a throne. I took the gold they thought was yours. I took your shields. You thought them dead. I bent so low to lift you up into a strange land. With a laugh they shook the earth. You did not know that who I love must let go of kith and kin, of friend and foe, and stand alone, bereft of land they call their own.

"A child at heart, you do not know the road I make for you to go. It is still long, with many bends. You see, you have to give yet a bleeding heart that bleeds to death for me."

Journey   *November 1952*

"When you threw shoes this way and that, I gave thy feet the wings they needed to rush, to fly on your journey into my Heart. It is so long, and you so small. The wings as yet do not have their full space. They will grow as you go over the land that you must pass to find my Heart.

"You are so small, so slow, so full of fears. Yet you must go alone, or so it seems. Behold this bend. It is as sharp as sharp can be. Arise, and hasten my love, my dove. For this is the time of trials, the time for tests my Father gives, my Father wills for all the souls that I desire with a desire of holy fire.

"Beyond the bend lies a wasted land of stones and fire. Arise and go into it. This is the time of tests and trials. My Father willed it so! This is his time. He is permitted to work his will and try his wiles on you who are so small and so alone (it seems).

"Beloved, stand still and understand. This is my Father's will that you be refined in fire, not seven times but seventy times seven. You are my steel and my steel must be clean of dross, unshakable, yet pliant like a sapphire. And fire alone can make it so.

"Go into the fire of his desire beyond the bend and let it burn until I blow it out with a glance. It is permitted that he should tempt you, entreat you to walk, to run, to go. But you stand still in his fire, and let it try to scorch where it will. It is my Father's will it be so.

"Stand still, and let the cold he breathes envelop you. Stand still, and let the fire of his glance touch you as it will. If you stand still, the fire will die, the cold thaw at your touch, the wine change into the white of new born snow. Behold I love you so! And yet I come to do my Father's will. And you are to be my steel refined from dross a thousand times or more.

"You did my work well. Slowly you built my house, brick by brick, of tears and pain and loneliness supreme, and darkness dark, and a million fears. You did my work well, my love, and I placed your house and you under my Mother's gown. Behold its white so stiff and stately sequined with stars, the bodice crimsoned from the touch of red, red wings. Your house is safe beneath her bridal robes.

"And yet, for you, this is the time of rest. But if you pass, I will give them my thirst for souls. Arise now and go beyond the bend. My love, my dove, stand still. This is my command. You will be obedient to it no matter what.

"Arise and go. You are so small. But you will grow into tempered steel without dross that will be used to fight for souls for whom I died in passionate embrace with death.

"For only I can do these things, I, the Lord thy God. And now I want souls who are pure. Rest, pray, restore my world to me, for I delight in nothingness that is humility. And I take my rest in selflessness. But you must be still now, beloved. For such is my Father's will, and hence my own.

"Cease asking. Be still as death and you shall know what life is like and its full delight. Then you shall know, but not before. But this I'll tell: I chose you for my own before you were. And yet, I made thee free, and let you run. You went and fell and fell again. And yet, for thee I died of love, and stood a beggar at thy door.

"You were so small, my child, my bride. You ran again and fell into the dust, the mire. And I was there to pick you up and make you white and clean again. And then you heard my love and you arose and came. And now *you are mine!*

"Be still, oh foolish child! Someday you shall see the souls you gave to me, and you will know they are of my humility. I came and walked the earth in search of such as you. I delight in washing clean, in making whole, and changing beauty for ugliness. Come here and nestle by my side, you foolish child.

"Of course you can speak to thy Love. Love can speak,

and love can wrap itself in silence. For love is God, and you his child, his spouse, his steel, his dove. And he can bid his angels comb your hair. Yet, you remain his nothingness.

"I speak, and you forget so soon, oh foolish child. I said I did delight to use the smallest things to wound his giant pride, but you forgot. Remember now, pay heed. You are what you are. I am Who is. The distance is infinity; the answer is eternity. As yet you are in time. I fashion you for timelessness. You are finite, but I mold you for infinity. My grace is enough for both.

"I shall not tell until time and eternity meet. And it will be no more of the whys and wherefores of my choosing you."

Oh love, oh God, oh Christ my Lord, I am confused, I am alone—poised for flight and on all sides the woods are dark, the night is cold, the road is grey. In rain and sleet, I, so small, am all alone. Forgive me, Lord. Crouched in the dust, I beg for faith to cover me and lead me on. Faith pure and strong. Faith in the light, faith in the dark, the grace of faith that stands very still wherever the Lord commands to stand!

The Road Is Grey   *November 3, 1952*

"The road is grey and dark. I know; I made it so. The night is filled with sleet and rain, and full of cold. I know; I made it so. Fear lurks in woods that frame the road and stand so stark, so very dark. I know; I willed it so.

"You are so small, oh foolish heart, and yet you fit my hand well and nestle there. Once again I say arise and go unto the road so wet, so grey, so dark. Arise and go into the night and meet the cold and sleet, for I delight in using the smallest things to crush his pride.

"You are a prize beyond compare for his black desire.

Yet, to reach you he must bend low as the grey, wet, dark road you walk at my desire. I watch him fight his foolish pride that will not let him bend so low. I take the night and fill it with rain and cold and sleet which he likes. It cools, he thinks, that fire I commanded to burn him. The fool! He does not know that sleet and rain and cold are but my fuel to his flame.

"You are a prize beyond compare for his insatiable desire. He will bend low to pick you up. But he will find that I am lower, and that there is no road, there is no grey, there is no dark. For where I am, thy loving God, all is light, warmth, and delight.

"You are so small, oh foolish heart, and yet you fit my hand well. When he bends for you, it will be there, yet you will not know then that it is so. For I delight to use the smallest things to crush his pride. And you *are* small, my nothingness.

"The night *is* cold, the woods *are* dark, and there *is* rain and sleet. Arise again! Go forth into the land of fears. For there is much for you to do, for Me, amongst the living and the dead tonight. Go forth and make the dead alive. Bring them from twilight into the light made whole because you went obedient to my word into the land of fears and met there Pride alone (or so you thought).

"Don't stop, don't run. Walk the slow and graceful walk of all small things that have to stand on tiptoe to reach on high. I know the night is cold, the road is grey, the woods are dark, and you are all alone (or so you think). But then, behold, dear heart, myself and him against the wood, the road, the sky, forever fighting for some soul.

"Walk slow and stand still when I command. For you are so small; you fit my hand so well. I will bend low, as low as you bent in humility, and use your smallness to crush his pride.

"Walk slowly into my night that seems so dark, so grey,

so cold, so full of rain, into my pain that sears and burns.
Someday, beloved, you will know that night was day, that
dark was light, that rain was . . . and sleet was. . . ."

Descent   *November 7, 1952*
                                         After 3 p.m.

"Descend, descend, you who are small. Descend, descend, and see what the face of despair looks like to me.
   "Don't touch. Just look and see. Men think despair is
dark. No, it is light, cold, deadly light and very bright.
   "Men think of death and peace when they see its lights
that look to them like distant stars at night. What they
don't know is that despair is a star very bright, but not of
my light nor of my heaven.
   "Descend, descend, you who are small, and see how
false despair looks to me.
   "When men run from the wounds I send to them to
make them grow, into its unpeace they think is peace,
then indeed they die all deaths and even I cannot restore
them to life.
   "Oh yes, I know. I killed your joy and would not let you
wake it, but bade you leave it on a floor littered with dead
leaves and waked by my wind.
   "You were so small and so alone. Indeed you were. For
I could not let my Lady Pain bring these to me and ecstasy; I was so sad. But today you had to plummet all the
way and see what despair is to me.
   "You felt its deadly cold. It imprisoned you in ice. But
you were still, obedient to my will. So now, arise and see
that you, so small, held men you'll never know from
touching its killing light.
   "Alone and cold, bereft of light, you were delight to
me.
   "And what is more, I will keep your joy a little longer

away from you; because, you see, emptiness and nothingness so pleases me.

"But rest at peace, my child, my bride. It won't be long,
and you will come to hide in a small wound of mine. You
are too small for others yet. And there I shall give you
soon to drink of wine that flows from there. And you will
know the taste of hope and faith. And I will give you my
bread to eat. And you will know how sweet is love.

"Today you saw despair and stood so still; and so kept
men you will never know until you see them in my heart,
my sacred wounded heart.

"Yes, I'll keep your joy a little more, for nothingness
and emptiness so pleases me."

Priests   *November 8, 1952*

"It has to be. And you must see a little—not much.
Because it is reserved for those I call my sons, my own,
for those who are before my Father's face.

"It is that dark, it is that stark, that those who are the
sheep, the flock, cannot partake of this, my Passion's inner core. It's a bitter draught this cup I give to them who
are my very own, nay, who are Myself!

"But you must see a little. You must catch a glimpse of
my dark sky, and just begin to understand the rim of my
dark, stark agony, which I give to make them strong, to
drink my cup to its last dregs, its galling, bitter dregs that
made Me sweat my precious Blood.

"Yes, they must go, my chosen ones, my own anointed,
called by my Father to be myself on earth—go into the
darkest darkness, the vomits of utter sin, and lie therein,
as I did lay, alive, but dead with all the deaths of all the
agonies.

"Yes, I reserve so much of what is mine to mine, and to
do so I permit, again and again, that those I love so much

will suffer from the hands of others whom I love like them, but who love Me not. The eternal Judas—the shining, clinking, silver pieces for Me, in them. Or who deride and maim, or kill or try to kill, with hands anointed by my Blood, my Word, Myself, in those I love who are like them.

"Behold my Father's anger like thunder! I show you but a glimpse, for no one can see and live, knowing the Father's anger. Behold its dark and just and heavy thunder, poised to strike the head and members. And I stand above and bleed more pain. And you so small must behold my Father's anger and my bleeding, precious Blood, and take the weight of both.

"So arise, my love, my dove so small, and stand. Atone! I will it so!"

My Growing Foolish Heart   *November 13, 1952*

"Yes, it is I, my little foolish heart, that grows so fast in love of Me. You cannot see that foolish you may be, but sweet, beloved. Lo, behold, and see thy heart expand, expand, to hold much more of Me.

"True, I can make Myself so small that, like a Baby, I can lie within the crib of any heart that starts to love Me as it should. But I desire, with flaming, mad desire, to grow until I fill their expanding hearts, leaving room for nothing but Me. For I am a jealous God. Alone, I can possess what came from my Father's hands, and for which I paid in full.

"Yes, it is I, my growing, foolish heart that fears, I who let all fears come to thee, overflow upon thee; yet, you stand so still. I rest in such a stillness that comes from faith.

"Yes, it is I, my Russian heart. I stand and watch the darkness that I allowed to come slowly engulf thee, until I know you cannot hear or see or feel or know that I am near. I eat so hungrily of the meat of your obedience, then feel refreshed by it.

"Yes, it is I, my nothingness, who holds the warm, all-embracing fire of my desire in check, and lets thee feel the icy cold of him, my foe, who hates thee so. You see, the fire of your love, I trust and use it to alleviate my burning thirst for souls. When *you* are cold, then the foe will come and make thy newly sown garden dead again. Then they arise and seek Me in the burning fire of their newly awakened, hot desire for Me.

"Yes, it is I who permits that you, my chosen one, my bride, be buffeted by his wind of price. And it is I again that lets him use his deadly intellect on yours. I watch, you moan; I watch, you bend this way and that. And then I watch you die a thousand deaths of doubts and come to life again—and die again and live in the agony of fears. Until you touched again the rim of cold and dark despair, yet stand still, and do not try to enter its eternal death, because your eyes are blindly, yet trustingly, fixed on mine.

"Then I arise in all my love and pay you back in ecstasy for resting Me when there was no resting place, for feeding Me when hungry. I was left to die outside a thousand, million doors. For giving Me to drink when parched. I broke and cried, *sitio!*

"Yes, then I arise in all my love and come to thee, beloved, whose heart expands so fast in love of Me. I come and fill it to the brim. You know when. For then my seal I break and enter thee, an arrow of eternal ecstasy.

"You see, beloved, the seal is gone, and in its stead I left a gaping, bleeding, sweet wound of love that you and I alone as yet can see.

"Yes, it is I. And I will come again. You will not know when, nor how, but you will wait forever, now that you can touch the wound I made in thine own heart."

My Heart Is Very Still *November 19, 1952*

My heart is very still today, waiting for I know not what, nor whom.

My heart is very still today, all hushed as if in strange expectancy, I know not for whom or for what.

My heart is very still today, immersed in a strange darkness shot through with lights that come and go like lightning, and blind me when they come, but leave the darkness darker when they go.

My heart is very still today, still with its utter emptiness that waits to be filled, but by whom? Or with what? I do not know.

My heart is very still today with the stillness of utter watchfulness that seems to listen, listen with each heartbeat. For whom? For what? I do not know. But it never listened so intensely, so intently, as it does now.

My heart and I are still today with a stillness of utter tiredness that seems to come from heaven and from earth and meet in us. There is no spot within my heart, my tired, wounded heart, that does not cry out for rest. There is no part of me that is not filled with pain. It is so great, the need for rest, that only utter stillness keeps us alive, my heart and I.

My heart is still today as if it had returned from a journey into eternity, or from one into the bowels of the earth, or into souls. The heights or depths have left my heart bereft of all things that hearts live by, and left it only stillness as a standby.

My heart is very still today, empty, and still waiting, full of a strange tiredness, filled with expectancy for something it cannot see, nor know, nor even touch. Poised in a void, it beats its rhythmic beat in utter stillness, a strange, unearthly symphony that somehow blends God and man and earth and heaven into one.

My heart and I are still today, and utterly devoid of all

curiosity, steeped in indifference, in strange abandonment. We stand so still, so still, and wait, for what, for
whom? Neither my heart nor I can tell.

My heart is still today with the strange stillness of a
love that is content to be in pain, in joy, in heaven, on
earth, alone, together, filled, empty, in turmoil, or rest.
One thing we do not understand, my heart and I: How
can emptiness be filled as we are filled, and yet be emp-
tier than emptiness, and wait and wait to be filled with
what, with whom?

My heart and I are still today because there is no
strength in us to move. We are condemned, it seems, to
stand so still that we can fool him who lives on noise.

My heart and I are still today. For one thing, we know
that we shall have to meet in stillness (which contains all
strength) Him who knows stillness not. He seeks my
heart and me today, and we shall have to pay in greater
pain for someone who wasted pain; and we shall have to
pay in silence for one who did not know that words are
servants of the Lord, our God.

My heart is still today with the stillness of emptiness
that will be filled when, how, by whom, or with what? It
does not know.

His Delight   *November 21, 1952*

Today my heart and I live in the light of God's own
Son. We move in it, and in it we breathe and have our
being. Its heat is in us, giving it back to the cold earth,
only to be filled again, until my heart and I are all light for
his delight.

My heart and I are strong today, with the strength of
love that came to us from the Crimson Dove, that covered
us with the alcove of its infinite spread of flaming wings,
while the Son kissed me with the kiss of his lips that went

through my heart in exultant ecstasy and first made us weak with love, and then made us strong again.

My heart and I are mad with the madness of love. We dance away upon the clouds and then come back again and dance our joyous mad dance upon his heart that opens up and takes us in, and makes us still in mad expectancy.

My heart and I are drunk today on the strong wine of love. And we live but to give the wine we had to all who thirst. We are so filled with it that it must spill or drown us in its sweet drunkenness that is the essence of sobriety and yet is born of a passion that takes its roots in his.

My heart and I are full today, for we were fed the Bread of Life. And we must, my heart and I, be eaten up, or we shall die of love.

Somewhere along the way I lost my heart and lost myself. For I was lifted up and became so beautiful that even I myself could not behold myself and live.

Somewhere along the way I ceased to be and was absorbed into a kiss, and felt the weight of him who is my God and my All. And I knew that I was not, but that he himself lived in me.

Today I know that I am beloved by him who brought me out from the dust of the earth and sent me from eternity into the thing called time, to dwell therein until again I shall return whence I came—this time his bride.

Today I know that my marriage bed, until then, is made of wood—plain, unadorned, naked as he and I. And yet, because of love, he descends, and then adorns the wood and makes it soft as dawn and fleecy clouds. And reaching high, unnails me, and lays me down and lets me know how soft a cross shared with him as a marriage bed can be, and how a mortal can know divine ecstasy and live to bring a ray of its delight to earth.

Today my heart and I are wise because wisdom penetrated us, himself in love.

Maria   *November 22, 1952*

Strange are my days—today—for I have no yesterdays and tomorrows never come to me. I live forever, or so it seems, in your translucent, iridescent *today.*

Strange are the ways of your today that stretch out, an immense and infinite and endless way to you.

Strange am I myself, a woman made of clay, of dust, and yet filled with divinity and grace. Strange indeed beyond the ken of most who walk the earth.

Strange to myself who spend so much of human time walking the dark labyrinthine ways of fears and doubts; and then suddenly to be embraced by the wind of your desire, and lifted up, up into the light that is no light, but you, my Lord, my rest, my spouse, my all.

I know you hide the light from me that you are, for I am not as yet of your eternity. And yet it dazzles me, such as it is, hidden from me and oh, so soft.

Yet not content to let the wind of your desire bring me from darkness into light, you take me, dust and clay, and lay me down unto your breast, and there I hear loud and clear the heartbeats of my God.

Strange are your ways, strange my todays. For I arise and walk and breathe and talk and live on earth; and all the while my heart, my soul, my mind and I, live in your light and hear your song of love. But, stranger still, my human lips know the kiss of your mouth.

Oh Christ, Oh Lord, my Lover and my God, how can this be, that I live in time and in eternity? My Beloved, why don't you send your most beautiful angel of death to me; for even without my yesterdays, and bereft of my tomorrows, today seems endless in my desire of you.

But no, forget I spoke, my Love. For to me there is but one ecstasy—to do your will. So let it be, today, forever, if you so wish, and let my exile continue until you alone will end it.

Oh Lord, what shall I say, I who have my being in the tumultuous way of your love, yet more amongst men who live on earth.

Behold me, Lord, a piece of clay, less than a handful of dust, and yet your bride, your spouse. My days are full of sheer delight, and then of utter pain, and then of lightness that becomes a darkness to be changed again into the grey and heavy in-between, that leaves me suspended in agony against a void of betwixt and between.

Now I know the warmth of joy of your caress. Then suddenly I am alone, and seek and run to find you here and there and everywhere, and cannot see a trace of you anywhere.

Then you know that I arise and go to touch you in the sick, the halt, the lame, the blind, for there alone I find you.

How strange is my today, Beloved, and yet I would not wish it otherwise. Behold me, Dove, I am all yours. Surrender is my name. I live but to do your holy will. Behold I am all love.

So lift me up into your light, or drop me into utter darkness. Forget me, pick me up and let me fall. No matter what, I am your slave and you my King.

Free As The Wind   *November 24, 1952*

My heart and I are free today, as free as air, as free as wind, as free as wild things are in wilderness, as free as a carefree youth who stands so straight, so young on the doorsteps of life. My heart and I are all that freedom is today.

And yet my heart and I remember yesterdays and know in some strange, mysterious way that we were bound and chained in our yesterdays.

My heart and I are wise today, for we know now how to be free, entirely free like the wind, the air, the wild things that live in wilderness.

We know that to be free like them, like this, we must surrender to the kiss of love, nay to the Lover who is our Lord and God.

My heart and I are wise today, with a wisdom that came to us from above, borne on the crimson wings of our Dove that comes to us whenever our Love sends it to make us wise; with wisdom that lifts all things of earth and throws them for an instant far away, then lifts us—my heart and me—beyond the ken of knowing and of mind, into the cloud of unknowing where dwells all wisdom.

Yes, my heart and I are wise today. For we are freer than the seas, the winds, the wild and warm things that dwell in wilderness. We are free as utter surrender can make us free. For now we move, not we, but He!

You Waste Your Time, Satan   *November 26, 1952*

You waste your time, oh Satan, whose hell is his eternal memory of heaven. Who hates all that reminds him of what he lost. Like shimmering white satin that clothed a transparency called Lucifer. Like blue that marries white so well and changes suddenly into a pair of eyes that caught the fire of all the blues the Lord lavished on earth and heaven, and then gave to her who bore his Son and crushed your head. Who in her utter childlikeness, slenderness, and youth, is like an army arrayed against you that you fear. And fear begets in you that hate which makes you now a puny wind or then a roaring lion. Who seeks but to devour, but whose growl is the meowing of an alley cat to those who are her slaves and know the secret of her immaculate and burning heart.

You waste your time, oh Satan, trying to move me from my destiny. Behold, my stronghold is his will. In it I lie obedient and still. Behold my hands, my heart, my soul, and how empty hands and hearts and souls can be of anything except him who conquered death and thee.

You love the dark. Black is thee, even in thy satanic

translucency. But you will take the dirty grey of a twilight on a rainy day. You think you can disguise yourself and be the night, the twilight. No. You waste your time, because you see, I know what heaven thrown into its own hell smells like. It smells like foul waters that once were crystal clear but now are stagnant, filled with hate and pride, imprisoned in the ice, the dirty, greyish ice, colder than cold itself, of memories, of whites and blues in which once you moved in your translucency.

Behold this clod of clay that moves within the Most Holy Trinity. Behold these eyes that will some day be naught but dust again. They see so deep, and their gaze is always inward, for they look only upon one face, His, who conquered death and thee.

You waste your time with me, and yet, make no mistake, I am as watchful as love can be. For I know that you have set snares for me. You hate me, Lucifer, who was an angel of light. And so I pray. You know I never cease. For prayer is man's speech with God in silence or in words. I use them both. A shield against your wiles as I make use of Jesus' and Mary's holy names.

You waste your time. And yet I know you must prowl like a restless beast, seeking a prey. For restlessness is you. All right, oh Satan of the dark and of the dirty greys. I, Catherine, a piece of clay, will fight thee with my lover's strength and Mary's power. Fight thee for the souls of all the sons of my Beloved's love—the man we call St. Francis of Assisi. It is the will of him who is my Lord and God, and so it is my will.

Beware! For hence, where I walk, God walks. And yet, since he permits, come on! Let us see who shall possess St. Francis' priests—you, or He?

Miserere   *November 27, 1952*

Miserere. My heart and I live in the depths. Miserere.

The depths are full of life that is the spawn of hell. Miserere.

And we must stand and let the spawn of hell touch us with its hot, dead, foul hands and never flinch. Miserere.

Because my heart and I are in depths not for ourselves but for those who once did hear his voice and went and left all things and followed him. Miserere. And then halfway along the road did worse than Judas. They did not sell him for silver or for gold; they made believe they still were all his own, but they allowed their hearts to go away from his. And so the bread he gave to them to give the little lambs and sheep turned to stone. Miserere.

Because of this, my heart and I live in the depths and cry and cry. Miserere.

Because of shepherds who wear clothing of a sheep and yet are wolves that prey and drink without fear the wine he meant for them to assuage men's thirst, my heart and I live in the depths. Oh, miserere.

My heart and I will have to learn that the depths do burn with a strange light that makes all slimy and dead in its light. Miserere.

Nor can we close our eyes and sleep, my heart and I, and shut out the deadly light. No. We must stand there and behold the awful sight that happens in the hearts of men when they shut out his light from those who need its warmth in the night of their agony. Miserere.

My heart and I are finding out that depths are endless and that we must go ever lower, lower into its tiered pits. So now come on, my heart, and for his sake and that of our love for him and hence for souls, let us make ready and plunge into the depths that are so dark, so utterly without light, and stay there listening. Miserere.

Do you know, oh heart of mine, that you beat too fast at times and then fears enter in. Miserere. Behold what you have done, oh heart of mine—or was it you, Beloved, that let fear in, into the deepest depths of hell that we entered for love of you? Oh, miserere.

Behold, fast beating heart, we must endure now all the fears that come in the dark of earthly nights to those who shepherd shepherds and who, like Peter, did deny him before the maids and men around the fires of life, but do not weep like Simon did.

Be still, my heart, and let the waves of fear go over you. And then we shall atone for them whom men respect and who wear the livery of the Crimson Dove that sees their nights so filled with fears and their days so filled with apostasy, and who weeps and lets his wings fall down; for he can't make alcoves over men who live a lie all day and sleep in fear all night. Oh, miserere.

Hold on, oh tired heart, hold on. For now we must be clad for men and women before we can rest in his thoughts of peace. Oh, miserere.

Stand still and let the cold, filthy hands of all who dwell in the depths of hell lay upon us, for love of him who dwells upon the heights of Calvary, the raiments of power and of pride. Oh, miserere.

Yes, I know, oh strange, unruly heart, that this will crush us both, and that we shall lie in the slimy depths, all bloody and a mass of wounds. But then, you see, oh heart of mine, our miserere will pierce the skies and, like an arrow straight and light, land at the feet of him whom our Love calls Father.

And, then, perhaps, he will unbend and give to her who bore his Son the ransom of his grace that will repay all things for which we went into the very depths of hell to pray our miserere.

Miserere: The Song Of Tears   *November 28, 1952*

Miserere. Miserere. My heart and I are still chanting the Miserere, the song of tears, of depths, of dark, of near despair. Oh, miserere.

We chant it when we have a voice. But then at times my

heart and I are voiceless. For when Lady Pain takes us into her strange embrace, the pain of it, the joy of it crushes all chant from us. And then we only say Miserere in an utter silence of the crushed, the dying, and those in pain. Miserere.

There are about my heart and me today the shreds of our yesterday. We seem to dwell in hell. And then, quite suddenly, we move into the kingdom of such blinding light that sun and moon and stars all pale and look so dull that we can look them straight in the eye and see them not. Miserere.

There is about my heart and me today a strange trans-lucency. We seem as if we were all free from ties of earth and flesh. And yet we are so still, so still. Oh, miserere.

For we hang, my heart and I, on a hard wood betwixt the earth and the dark sky, nailed fast. And our thousand wounds sing our Miserere, because *we* can't.

The wood is high upon a hill. The nails bite deep. But we can see so far, so deep, much deeper than the nails bite in our flesh. Oh, miserere.

The nails tear up my flesh. My back is like a flame of pain. My heart knows what thorns feel like when stuck into matted hair. My heart is open like a door and bleed-ing, bleeding all the more. Oh, miserere.

But my heart and I see far and deep and cry for more. For what are nails that tear or head that knows the pain that eats and eats some more! What matters a flaming back of pain when down there alone, in white, a father weeps and cries at night—Miserere.

Oh nails, bite deeper. Oh wood, be harder. Oh pain, flay more. Let all of me burn and be consumed. Let my heart die from blood and love; but let the father of Chris-tendom cease to weep in the dark night alone, and let his words pierce human hearts like darts of love; and let those who are his very own and show his face to all his sons in distant lands arise and feed their flock, standing up, like good shepherds should, and not lie down in downy beds and make believe that they are bishops of their flock. Oh, miserere.

They fool everyone but him who sees the tears of him who is his vicar on our forlorn earth. Oh, miserere.

My heart and I are almost dead from pain. And yet we haven't even begun to drink the bitter draught of his passion. Oh, miserere. So take a deep breath, oh wounded heart, and start to learn what was the price he paid for you. Oh, miserere.

Oh do not fear, my little heart. You see, fear has left me all weak in his love. I just lie still and take the imprint of his will as it comes. For in his will is life and love and ecstasy. Oh, miserere.

But you and I will ask for naught but what he wills. For this is the time to pay and pay and start again, for pride and sloth, for wasted words and wasted pain. Oh, miserere.

This is the time to pay for gold and lust and love of power, all spawns of hell. This is the time to chant, to whisper or to bleed—Miserere.

We are so small, so weak, my heart and I. But we can know the kiss of pain and bleed to death for our Love—Oh, miserere.

So arise, my fearless heart, and let us go, nay run, and meet the depths of hell, the heights of light, the kiss of God, the touch of slimy, dead, and bloated things, the waves of fear, the kiss of pain, the bite of nails, the feel of thorns; and through them all sing our Miserere, because it will—don't ask how—answer his cry: Sitio!

Pilloried *December 2, 1952*

My heart and I are pilloried today on the big square of life. It is so lonely there and yet so bright.

We do not know why the stocks; we do not know why this time, this place. All that we know, my heart and I, is that human eyes are dead and cold when gazing at our helplessness, and that they slap us in the face with their looks and their stares and make us dizzy with a strange pain that was not there yesterday.

Again my heart and I are dumb with strange stupidity that numbs us deep. Yet we submit to a curiosity that claws and whips us with a whip that whistles like they do in hell before it falls on both of us, my heart and me.

We stand stock-still because we must, but we know not why. Yet it hurts and hurts us endlessly in spite of love that fills my heart and me.

We know the fact, my heart and I, that men will hate us till we die; some men, that is, to whom we are a hated sign.

We know some more, my heart and I. We know that other men will love us even after we die. For they too will behold a sign in us that they have looked for long and far.

We stand so still, my heart and I, and let the cold stares of human eyes tear our face apart, and then bend our back to meet the whip that forms on their lips so full of froth curiosity begot.

But that is but a start. To finish is yet to come. It will make us a thing of shame, all broken, mangled, a bloody mess all filled with dirt from boots that kick and hands that hurt.

No one will chant a requiem over us except the wind, the stars, the moon. We shall not need it, not at all, because by then we will be resplendent in him.

My Heart and I Sing Songs   *December 3, 1952*

My heart and I sing strange and changing songs these days. They come to us from far away. The tune is called from somewhere outside of us; the pitch is given. All we have to do is sing the songs.

My heart and I sing strange songs these days that keep

changing their melodies at times so fast that my heart and I get weary trying to catch up.

My heart and I sing songs these days that change so fast that we truly want to stop singing completely, but we can't, for the songs came from somewhere outside of us and we must keep singing their ever-changing melodies, no matter what.

My heart and I sing now a song of joy that changes in an instant into a song of pain, only to become again a song of light that suddenly throws us into the depths of pain and darkness.

How often must my heart and I sing with lips gone dry from thirst, and voices cracked with tiredness! We sing from depths where our voices come back to us like whips. We want to stop from searing, scorching flames of pain, but from somewhere outside of us we are bid to go on and sing our songs of pain.

And then, quite suddenly, we sing with joy, and our song soars right straight through all the blues of heaven to his wounded Heart, and nestles there with all its tender notes like so many love-darts.

But oh, the pain of singing well! We are stretched out and torn apart, asunder, and nails bite deep into our hands and feet. And a lance kisses with its sharp spear and tears our flesh some more, and wounds our souls so deep.

But sing we must, my heart and I, from depths, from heights, from everywhere. Our Love bids us to sing our song of desire, joy, tears, pain, fears, that all add up to a melody of love. It seems our songs go very far, and make men stop and listen to them within their hearts, and suddenly hear in them the echo of God's voice in us.

Lord of my heart, we beg of Thee to help us to go on, no matter what, and sing those songs and chant those melodies that change so fast and are so strange, but make men's hearts listen to Thee. And please, Beloved, give us the grace to sing them when and how and where you wish!

My Heart Is Very Wise   *December 6, 1952*

My heart and I are very wise today, with the strange wisdom of little things that live in utter simplicity. My heart and I are very wise today because we spent our yesterday in the domain of Lady Pain. She holds there, in her domain, many strange and secret ways, and tales of how to become wise by lying still, by giving up one's whole will to him who is Wisdom in the flesh of man.

My heart and I are very wise today because we were so still and listened most attentively to what Lady Pain had to say; but mostly because we let her work her will in us and were not afraid to embrace her whom all men shun. And then she laughed and kissed us back, and from that hour we became wise in little things, unafraid of pain because of love.

My heart and I are wise today with the strange wisdom of simplicity that lacks curiosity and is so utterly devoid of impetuosity, that is, of self; but stand ready and willing to do the bidding of him who knows all things because he loves.

My heart and I are wise today with the strange wisdom of those who love utterly, totally, without holding back a single sigh, and who surrender body and soul, mind and heart, and stand apart from most men—because we are not like them, full of so many things but empty. For in truth, we are utter nothingness, we are emptiness that emptied itself because it did not know how else it could love; it had to love or die.

My heart and I are wise today because, being utter nothingness and emptiness, his pity came and led us into the depths of his flaming heart. And there his tenderness filled us with his choicest wine of love, so that now we are the strangest sight for angels and for men: nothingness and emptiness that is so filled that it must spill love, pity, and tenderness onto all those who hunger and thirst for him, yet find him not, because those who were meant to feed them, don't!

My heart and I are wise tonight, for our opened eyes see deep and far into men's hearts and souls, and then look up and with a glance, span time and then rest in eternity. But for human eyes to be so wise, my heart and I are crucified upon the wood that holds the love that burns so bright in our eyes, and makes them see beyond today, yesterday, and eternity.

We hang so high, and wonder how we got that way. And suddenly we think we know. This is how. It all began so long ago when we were small as men know time, and stood on tiptoes to kiss the feet of Christ, the King of the Jews, and tell him, as only children can, that my heart and I love him enough to always wish to be with him through life.

And all the people whom we called *big* shook their heads and spoke quite low, saying that my heart and I will end our days all clad in black and schooled in love by convent ways.

But we went on our childish way, and followed him unto a hill where suddenly we became, my heart and I, quite grown up and very shy—yet innocent of heart and soul. It was a high hill, filled with sun that kisses the flowers on his run. But we had little time to learn how flowers kissed the sun in ecstasy.

My heart and I were looking up, and so our Love came striding back to us across the vivid blue, with Giant's stride, and knew that he would reach us soon, as God reckons time. He reached us, true, but not to stay and kiss our joyous tears away. No. He came to offer us the gift of making his way of the Cross with him.

Love knows no age. My heart and I jumped up and cried our *fiat* with arms flung wide against the sun, the wind, the blue of the whole sky. And then began our descent into the dark of terror, fear, and bleak monotony of pain. How well my heart and I remember when we followed him to Gethsemani. It was not his garden, and yet it was. There were no olive trees, no Jewish hordes.

There was just us, and Him, and a chalice immense and bitter that he bid us drink to the last drop. How many years did it take us, my heart and I, to drink it dry?

But drink we did. And then men came and took us to the square of a big city, and flagellated us with whips of fear and whips of death—not ours but the death of those we loved. And when my heart and I lay bleeding in the dust, as if all dead, they picked us up, and suddenly, somehow, we were far, far away, across tumultuous seas, amidst more men who put on our bloody head a crown of thorns, all woven of poverty abject, and misery too deep for words—ignominy, that held so fast, as it does, all the despised poor everywhere. And then again the ships, the sea of water and misery, and then the New Land.

This put on my heart and me a cross that seemed to tower so high over our littleness that for a while we could not move from where we fell when we saw it. Yet, with his help, we lifted up the Cross that would have broken us; but he held it and led us up a strange and naked hill that seemed to tower over the whole world we lived in.

And there men tore all our bloody clothes with their claws and deadly curious eyes, and nailed us naked upon the wood. Then lifted it up with us, my heart and me.

That is how we come to see so far, so deep, across all time into eternity. Eyes get that way when Love has its way with hearts and men; and they, like us, surrender all and follow Love upon its throne of utter pain.

Dead Grass   *December 17, 1952*

My heart and I are in a plain of pain today. It is so flat, so flat, that it seems endless and limitless.

It is a plain of gray and brown, full of dead grass that makes a strange and plaintive sound when my heart and I touch it with our steps.

The sound grows and so does the plaint. And we stop
and take it in and know that sound can wound my heart
and plaint can pierce my flesh with a thousand darts that
make it bleed without blood, that make it cry without
sound.

The plain is endless; so is our pain.

But what is this plain of gray and brown that doesn't go
up or doesn't run down, but stays as flat, as straight, as if
it were made by careful hands that planned it flat, as flat
as that?

Oh foolish heart, oh little love! Can you not see that I
have sent you into the plains of indifference and tepidity?
It is not a plain of pain. The pain is mine. I loan it to you
just for today. For don't you see? I want it verdant, fruitful, full of rolling hills and little valleys, where I can build
on rock and not on sand.

Oh foolish heart, you walk in pain so that the plains of
men's indifference, tepidity, may flower with the flower of
fire which is their love of me.

I gave you pain to make it rain my graces on the brown
gray of human strange tepidity. Today still has some time
to live. And so, keep on and walk my arid plains and
bring me back fertility.

Silence and Atonement   *December 19, 1952*

My heart and I have learned silence today. It took us
very long to understand that silence is part of the domain
of Lady Pain. That there are courts and stairs and turrets
and chambers without end in the domain of Lady Pain.

And my heart and I, as we grow, will slowly and
surely—(because we are yet fairly small and not quite
learned as yet in all the ways of pain and love)—spend
some time in every court, and walk each steep step of
every stair and enter turrets, chambers, one by one, and

stay in each, until each one has taught my heart and me its lesson of pain, its chant of love.

And then some day, we do not know when, my heart and I will find the last strange ladder that will bring us to final ecstasy and death that starts a life of endless and eternal delight.

But that is not yet. For we must learn to suffer and to wait, to hide from all the facts that now we live in two domains, that of earth and that of Lady Pain.

We are so slow, my heart and I, to learn anything at all. And yet today we learned the art of silence when in pain. We learned that the skins of a white doe bind tight and that they increase the pain a hundredfold. Yet silence must be kept. We tried so hard today when we were crucified.

And now we know that pain borne for love's sake is like a flame that brings us into the very heart of pain and then dips us into the infinity of peace that sends us back again into the heart of pain.

Yes, silence taught us much today. We learned that love must have is way and never count the cost. We paid the cost in silence and in joy while in the very heart of pain.

I Swing   *December 26, 1952*

My heart and I are on a swing today, and were also all yesterday. We swung to joy and joy swung us back to pain so fast we did not even know how or when we were back with pain again. And pain gave us a kiss and made us faint, and then swung us to joy fast back again.

My heart and I swing to and fro and do not care which way we go, because the hand that swings the swing is his. We are content to swing and swing between the depths, the heights, the stars, the night, for we know what lies in store for us.

Today we saw the map of our strange journey inward of darkness and light, that started somewhere in the past, we have forgotten when. Perhaps it was when we played with Christ at the age of five. It does not matter any more. We know we are his bride, my heart and I, that our marriage bed is cruciform and very hard.

We know that we must learn fast to love as perfectly as he who wills us soon, when we are ready, to mount his throne of wood and pain and lie there in utter ecstasy within the circle of his nailed hands.

For then and only then will we become his very own in that strange kingdom of love and joy that knows no time, no cross, nor pain, but only the fullness of the Lamb so cruelly, so utterly slain for us.

Oh hurry up, my laggard heart. Let us begin to climb and climb. Behold the hill is far away and love is calling us night and day.

O hurry up, laggard heart. Oh hurry, hurry, don't make him wait.

A Child And Silence   *December 26, 1952*

The heaviness is heavy with all the weight of pain. And yet the exultant sings its passionate alleluias; and then goes utterly beyond all sounds into the heart of praise, which is a silence that sings its song with the voice of God himself, that strangely comes from the very souls of men.

The heart is pierced by love and bleeds and bleeds, unseen, unknown, its song of pain that is in truth a song of final joy, the cry of a soul that sees the gates of heaven open in a Child's eyes.

The soul is watchful like a concentrated entity that centers utterly on a helplessness that holds all power, encompasses the unencompassable, surrounds eternity, and hands it to time that lifts up high the Child who cut it out for man to hope, believe, and love, so that he could again return whence he came, to that eternity.

The mind is stilled before the sight of wisdom become a Child. It knows without understanding how wisdom is found when all knowledge is left behind, except such as comes from keeping watch before a little Child lying in a crib and playing with his toes.

And all around and about, a shadow powerful and sweet falls on the walls, the Child, the soul, the mind, the heart; a strange young shadow, barely fifteen, that sings a soft song to the Child and makes the angels and such men as listen know silence so completely that they can catch and hold the voice of God and know Love incarnate is small, so small their hands can hold it; so can their hearts. But only if the heart will grow as does God's voice and love who is his only Son.

For Priests   *December 28, 1952*

My heart and I are poised today on the rim of loneliness and pain. It is a narrow rim—the ledge is thin—and we shall not be able to stand there long.

Yet ere we begin our descent, so slow, so measured, so full of darkness and of pain, we have—my heart and I—to drink a chalice of bitter wine.

Fear stalks nearby, and yet we stand as still as if we were the dead. For love's command rings loud and clear in our ears, and trust holds up faint heart and me.

And now the night is still, the house asleep. It is time to start descending into the deep.

With steady hand that love commands, we lift the cup and drain the bitter, galling draught that we must drink before we go into the well of utter loneliness and grievous pain.

For this is the allotted time, this is the time he named for us, my heart and me, to start using the double strength he sent so recently.

Behold, my heart, your task of love. You are the port, the shield that shelters God's priests and draws the light-

ning of God's thunder and anger from those who, blind
and deaf and dumb, dare touch his own anointed ones.

Fold down your thoughts so full of fear. Descend, descend, unto the end into the well of loneliness and pain.
Heed love's command.

I want it so, your Lord, your God. Now is the moment.
Arise and go. I wish it so.

Sharing the Passion   *December 30, 1952*

My heart and I are learning slowly the prayer of utter
silence that covers with its strange mantle all the new
bleeding wounds that seemed to have covered us these
dark, shining days!

My heart and I are learning slowly the weight of unshed tears that press us into the dust of the road of utter
loneliness. We travel slowly, painfully, these dark and
shining days.

My heart and I are learning the hidden prayer of pain
that lives with us all day and watches with us while we
sleep. There is in us a strange passion going on beneath
the days, the hours, the minutes, the seconds that go to
make what men call time!

We walk, we talk, we eat, we sleep, we work, we laugh,
and yet, my heart and I live all the while in Gethsemani!
And darkness, black, heavy-weighed, envelops us with
all its force.

And when we think that we will die because the weight
is crushing us, then suddenly my heart and I are wide,
alive, tied and strapped against a post of ornate wood.
And our flesh is torn! Is torn to bits by cruel whips until
we feel that we are but a flame of pain, and will dissolve
in its bloody sea. (Or is it a loving melody?)

But then, lo! Behold! My heart and I are walking
strange, steep streets, bowed down to the ground beneath

a cross of wood that opens up the thousand wounds the whips kissed into flame.

Yes, that is where we are, my heart and I. Today making the way of our passion, silently, while we speak and work and walk and eat and laugh. Oh Lord of pain and love, give us strength to keep on thus unto the end!

Days of Pain   *December 31, 1952*

There is a strange, compelling stillness about us, my heart and me, these days. And yet, within the core of us, there is a churning, moaning, hurling wind of pain.

It seems as if we are lifted high in mighty sweeps that crush the very breath and bones of our life. And then before we uttered a moan, a cry, we are thrown down against the rock that fills the very bottom of all the depths that ever were.

Behold us now, you who pass by, and see us walk and talk and smile and work. Behold us now all crushed, all broken up, a sack of bones rattling within the flesh that bleeds from a thousand wounds.

But you cannot behold us thus, my heart and me. Your eyes are held to our pain, your ears are closed to our moans. This time we must bear things that come from the mighty hand of God, alone, in utter darkness of naked faith, in utter stillness of obedience.

This is the time, these are the days allotted us, to die a thousand deaths and know a thousand wounds, a thousand pains. For this we got a double strength of food, that is not only food but love who is the Lord our God. For these are the days of standing still so that someone else may walk with strength.

These are the days of pain and wounds of darkness, edged with strange edges of fear so that someone else may walk without fear in utter light.

These are the days that must be borne in silence and with burning love for all who had to know the knife, the wound of spurned love, of love declined, reviled and spat upon.

These are the days that my heart and I must lift with hands that barely can hold them in their bloody wounds, the priests that have come down God's steps and left them for good, and went and got lost in the mist of Satan's wiles.

Stand still, my heart, and let the wind of God lift you high up and crush you down. You are with me his tool these days, so be still and quiet and take what comes.

Remember, it was his own command given to us by his own priest who said that God asked this of us with love and trust.

So here we are, my Lord, my God. Behold myself, so small, your nothingness. Behold my fearful heart, all emptiness, but ready, eager, willing to live or die at your own bidding, in any way, in every way your love, your trust commands us.

Journey Inward   *January 2, 1953*

My heart and I keep on our strange journey inward that began, it seems, long ago. We have forgotten much of the thousand roads that were, in all verity, one; forgotten that our weary, joyous, dancing feet traveled in the yesterdays that have gone into the hands of Mary, to be used as she, our mistress, wishes to use them.

Yet we know, my heart and I, that this strange journey inward will go on and on, until we come face to face with Him who started us on it. For He is both its beginning and its end. We do not know when that shall be. We are content, my heart and I, to keep on and on, making our journey inward, toward Him who once kissed us with the kiss of his mouth.

Yes, we are content to make the journey inward through all the pain, the searing, flaming pain, the dark, dank, stinking pain, the little sharp pain that comes from salt of tears that fall in millions of little wounds we seem to acquire as we go on, my heart and I.

And through the unspeakable, unexpressionable, all-embracing, all-gathering pain that eats through us like acid eats through steel, we know that all pain gives us my Love. All pains. For they are your cross and we, my heart and I, are filled with a love of it.

Yet, we do not really even ask for pain, but only for your sweet, divine, and holy will. In it we want to live, to move, to have our being. All else is bitter to our taste. All else is dross and dung. All else does not exist for us.

Oh, Lover! Oh, Beloved! We rest content to walk the road of our strange journey inward, through pain, through joy, through laughter, through tears, through darkness, through light, through all the endless delights, or none at all.

We'll walk it, my heart and I, even if we are crucified by your own desire! At your command, we'll walk it by standing still, or by being lifted up on the holy wood. Just say the word; just give your sign.

You know, oh Love, we are all thine, so utterly, so fully, that at times we seem to cease to be and change into surrender, obedience, and charity.

We know, my heart and I, that we are utter nothingness and emptiness. But now we know that you delight in such, in a way incomprehensible and strange to us of earth and clay!

And so we rest, content in emptiness and nothingness, and wait, as long as you desire, before your door. Wait for you to open it and come, come to fill us full with choicest wines of your divine cellars. And then we arise again and are more ready to face all the pains you wish to send.

Behold us, Lord, my heart and I. So constantly wounded with the arrows of your love. We are, we know, but wax that lives to receive the imprint of your seal, and then to arise to do your holy will.

You know, Beloved, that, in a way, we are completely dead, though yet alive. That truly, we live not but you in us, alleluia!

Crimson Red   *January 3, 1953*

"Be still, beloved, and know that I am loving thee today, in my own fashion. Behold, once again I open my treasure chest, and bring my gifts for thee. For you who have wounded my heart, I give the crimson red of pain. Stand still, my love, and let my loving, pierced, and bleeding hands bedeck thee this day in the vivid red that matches them.

"And here in white, snow white, you saw the weaving of this seamless garment (with which I desire to clothe thy nakedness before you put on the mantle of vivid red). Last night, when you drove into the bleakest night, you were filled with my blinding white, to meet me, thy Lover and thy God.

"Yes, I was there in poverty and pain. And you ministered to both with gentle hands and loving heart. That is why I let you know, on your way back, how sweet I am. You tasted of my grapes; they gave you choicest wine. Remember this, and know that your nakedness is now clothed in the white of snow. I want it so. I wove it for you last night. And now, you who loved much, are yourself white as snow, and warm beneath my mantle of crimson red.

"Stand still, my love. I must bedeck you yet in the grey gossamer of loneliness. It goes well with the gold of your hair! The snowy white, the crimson cloak. No, don't move. Be still as I bade thee.

"White, red, and grey become you well, my love! But you need a clasp to hold the crimson cloak. And so, behold a clasp of pearls that mirror the white, the grey, the red in their matchless depths.

"You know that pearls stand for tears. And so they do. And now, my love, my bride, you are bedecked in snowy white that makes you pure as light. So shine, and show souls the way to my loving heart that hungers, thirsts, seeks, and waits for them to enter in through nights and days.

"And now, my love, my bride, wear your cloak of crimson red as a queen should, with grace and dignity. And let no one know the weight of its excruciating pain. It won't be long. Its crimson will become a little redder from your own blood that will flow hiddenly and slowly from your wounded heart, wounded too with love for Me.

"Stand still, my beautiful one, and wait upon my will. For it may be that I will desire to dye my crimson cloak with deeper hues from other hidden wounds of yours. I want you so pliant, so obedient to my holy will, that you will stand still, all still, and be willing to accept whatever, whenever I will to send it.

"Bend down your head, my love. The grey that veils its gold needs gems to set it off. And a queen must be crowned by her King. Bend lower, child of my love and grace. Here is my crown of darkened thorns, with blood-red rubies set on their sharp ends to mingle with the ones whose shadow I have already given thee! And now, my love, my own, you do indeed resemble Me.

"Fear not. I will not touch the gold of your soft hair. No one but those I wish will see the white of snow, the red of blood, the grey of loneliness, the pearls of tears, the crown of thorns.

"No one will know that I wedded thee with a slender gold band that holds your hand in mine. It is time that you should know that you are mine and that I want from you utter surrender, perfect obedience, naked poverty, and a heart filled with the passionate, mad love of my cross, and Me. For whoever is mine has for his marriage

bed, at first, the cross. This is my wish for thee, Catharina
mea, whom this day I have clothed in the most precious
gifts taken from the hidden treasure chest of my wounded
divine and human Heart."

My Restless Heart   *January 4, 1953*

My heart and I are full of restlessness tonight. Yet we
stand still and fight, it seems, the demons of the night
that dance their evil dance all around us.

The voice of my Beloved knocks at the door of my
heart; but when I hasten to open it, he is not there. And
now I know the meaning of the canticles of love, for I
tremble with desire and feel I must arise and seek him
whom my heart loves. But I cannot, because obedience
has tied me to a spot of utter stillness.

He bade me, my Love, my God, to stand still and not
move until he gives me leave to cease being stiller than
death. And so I stand with all the demons of the night
dancing their evil dance around me.

And the door of my heart is wide open for him who
knocks at it, yet is not there; but whose knocking has left
me filled with the thousand flames of my desire for him
and the soft biting bands of obedience forbidding me to
seek him, without whom it seems I cannot live at all, at
all.

Miserere.

Christ Speaks   *January 5, 1953*

"Now you know, child from the distant land my
Mother loves, you know that it was I who spoke to thee.
That it was truly I who gave thee the white of snow, the
cloak of red. You felt its excruciating weight today and I
am glad you wore it with dignity as I bade thee to.

"The grey of loneliness enveloped you today. I know. I willed it so. You know you have to drink my cup. This is why you fell like a broken thing today, prostrated before me like one who is dead.

"I left you lie like that so that you may taste the dust, the grey, swirling dust, of utter loneliness I tasted on my way to Calvary.

"Your head was all a flaming fire of pain. I know. I willed it so. Did I not crown you with my own crown. Now you know how sharp are thorns.

"But you know more, because today your crimson cloak was dyed a darker hue. Nobody knew that it was so, but your blood flowed and dyed it that way.

"It came from hidden wounds. You did not see its flow yourself, but you felt the wounds grow deep and wide within your feet, your hands, your side.

"Today, the vigil of the feast in which I showed my face, my grace, to the gentiles, I choose to give you a taste of Judas' kiss, of Peter's lies that wounded me more than whip, more than the tree.

Keep standing still, wrapped up in white, in red, in grey. They do *so* become you child of a distant land my Mother loves. Keep standing still. Keep standing still. It pleases me.

Refrain of Pain   *January 6, 1953*

There is within my heart today a strange languidness. It seems as if I drift and drift like a dead leaf picked up along the field by an unexpected wind.

I know we are in pain, my heart and I, and the pain is only a refrain to the strange song of loneliness that someone sings within us so constantly.

We drift with all the currents of the swift, strange wind that picked us up, and watch the blood from our unseen wounds make a red trail down below, we don't know how.

We cannot think well today at all, my heart and I. We are awake and yet asleep somehow, we do not know quite how.

It seems as if, steeped in pain, in loneliness, we drift, we know not where nor how, from wind to wind in utter indifference.

Perhaps my heart and I are numb from all the excruciating pain that slept with us last night. We do not know quite how we got that way. It seemed last night we heard the voice of God; and yet perhaps we did not.

We went, my heart and I, to the house of our Love today. We went therein to pray, but instead he took us so far away that we became as transparent as light and lost our body somewhere in the night that we left behind.

We stayed in light, it seemed, for an eternity, and yet it must have been just an instant as men count time. For there we were kneeling in our pew, my heart and I, full of languidness, fluidity, and streams of blood that seemed to us his rays of love.

Right now, we drift and drift and cannot stop, and feel all pain and none at all. We wonder, my heart and I, if we are dead or alive and what befell us and when and how.

"Oh foolish heart that is so wise and yet who, it seems, will never understand the ways of my love. Come, rest upon my breast, and listen to my song of love.

"Because, you see, I have chosen you, child of a strange and distant land that mirrored so well my Mother's face in its crucified heart, to bring the image of that face to the fair land that knows her not and loves her less.

"That is why I took you from there and brought you here to this land my Father shaped with his own hand. That is why I put you through my school of love and called to you so many times, so many ways, in people whom no one would love.

"I tested you in many ways and now I test you again through pain.

"Oh foolish heart that loves me well in all the poor and in all men, of course you do not know why you drift like a leaf in utter languidness of growing love.

"You see, I wish it so. You must; you will undergo my passion and walk my ways from Bethlehem to Calvary. I will it so.

"But it is written that only love embraces pain and stands with a song in its wounded heart, ready to die for the beloved.

"Oh foolish heart, I am now teaching you the supreme ways of love; and they reduce you again to what you call my nothingness, my emptiness. Only now emptiness is filled with me and your nothingness is one with me who always is, was, and shall be.

"I am a jealous God and you are all my own. My priest knows that he is I to you. I charge him to guard you well and teach you the keys to what I want of you—utter surrender. He knows the locks, he knows the keys, he knows the pain that goes into fitting lock and key.

"Tell him for me to be merciful by being seemingly merciless with you in leading you to me with giant strides in the paths of love and pain.

"For I have need of you to show the face of my Mother that your Russian heart will reflect so well when it is utterly crucified like that of the land where you came from and which she loves so well.

"Now rest upon my breast, Mary's Catherine, and drift and drift like a leaf in the wind of my own love."

Love Is A Wind   *January 11, 1953*

Love lay so still within my heart today that I was like a cradle rocking it. Then love became a wind within my heart, so soft, so gentle, that I began singing its lullabies with it.

Then suddenly love was a wind within my heart, hot, dry, and filled with such a passion of desire that I became a pliant dancer to its tune. Then love arose in all its might and pierced me through with its delight until, in utter, passionate surrender, I touched its heart and vanished in its depths.

And now I am love's home, its cradle and its song; and yet I am as one who is not, because I vanished in its depths.

So how can one who is not bring love's song to other souls, become a cradle for their woes, a home for their homelessness? I ask you, Love, how can that be?

"I listen to your words, child of the distant land my Mother loves as does my heart. Rest silently and keep my words in yours.

"You are because you have your being in me, who was and is and shall be eternally. I made my home within your heart; and now it is so big that it must become the home of all the lost and homeless ones that roam the world in search of me.

"For don't you see, Catharina mea, a heart that for an instant held its God can hold the world and all therein and have space left for all the rest of the universe of spheres and stars and moon and sun.

"You said well—you are the cradle of myself, for I became a child to lie therein. But you remember well that I, a child, a youth, a man, am still the Lord your God. And if your heart my cradle is, then it can and must cradle all the woes of all the souls I send to lie therein as I did lie.

"Catharina mea, whose name and heart holds my song of love and lets it take you in its depths. I give my song to souls because I want it sung upon the earth. For how else would they know who dwell on earth, the depth, the height, the width, the breadth of the love song of their God?

"And so, bride of my heart, you are my song. Make no mistake; you will sing it until you die and it will be a song of ecstasy which is myself.

"To sing it well you will from hence dwell in the wind

of my desire that brings until the end the notes of pain, the notes of joy, the notes of ecstasy that come with constancy, that will make you sing a perfect tune because you will cease to be and I shall sing it with your voice.

"So now, make ready to burn in my desire, to die and die again in all my pain, and then bear the burden of my joy to burn again and die again. Amen. Amen. I have spoken."

Contradiction   *January 21, 1953*

Incoherent, prostrated, tumultuous, my heart and I *rest* in his love. How can this be that we stand up and yet are there prostrated, a senseless thing as still as trees before a storm, or waters without a ripple on the morn.

How can it be that we move with tumultuous grace through waves and waves of his creative love, and yet *rest* in it? How can it be, that we are so incoherent, in awe, and yet so simply at rest upon his breast?

We are a contradiction to ourselves! A thing of storms and of peace, of stillness and of movement swift, of incoherence and clarity supreme. Indeed, we are a leaf borne along on the current of his love.

And there we go again! Up, up into the light that is, was, and shall forever be. And now we plummet down, down, into the depths of hell, and know the slow begetting and conceiving, the carrying and delivering, of the monstrosity that springs from Lucifer's sterile fecundity— the *anti-christ*.

"Ascend, ascend, stay still, move on, follow my will. Descend, descend, die now a thousand deaths, and live again, die again, and be a chalice, be a bride, be little, empty, nothingness. Defy the foe—rest, arise, ascend, descend, be wise, be slow, move fast, stand still, see, be blind, descend, ascend, be simple, be all mine."

My heart and I are Yours my God. Behold us lying on the pierced palm of your hand. Content to ascend, descend, live, die, arise and go into all depths, come back again and lie in child-like trust and love to await your will's desire.

Iridescent light lifts us and then absorbs us again. We are and we are not. We know we love, so we must *be* before his face. We cannot see, we cannot know, and yet we do. Oh light that brings us to fecundity!

"Child of my love, lie still and know my will and be all impregnated with my light—for I am Light. I clothed you in the green of utter simplicity. Green is hope that rests in faith and dies for love—and lives again in everlasting simplicity of trust, the fruit of love.

"Simplicity is nourished by surrender, utter, complete, and instant! It feeds on dying to self. You are dead, and so clothed in the green of the simple simplicity of all the little, living things that die in hope and live in love.

"But I desire more pliancy in thee; and pliancy comes from obedience that is complete, unquestioning, and rooted in a readiness for more obedience no matter how incomprehensible or strange! I want that kind of pliancy, and I want it now!

"Love hungers for atonement; mine does. You need the meat of pain, the strength of suffering pain. You need to offer up body and soul in constant, unflagging atonement for those who make up the face of the anti-christ.

"This is my time! I want thee fashioned for my instrumentality, pliant and ready to assume what I shall send! Make thyself ready with the full readiness of saints. You know that means whip and lash, and hard boards for your sleep, and less and less to eat. We enter now into my noviciate.

"This will be the final test, for you must now put much to rest, and gather strength from love of Me, to make thee ready for my marriage bed—the Cross! For I will then lift thee up and bring through this uncounted souls to assuage my thirst! Amen! Amen!"

Bound

Incomprehensible, unfathomable, unsearchable, the ways of God encompass me.

Somewhere along the royal road I was bound with the skins of a young doe that were worked to complete pliancy and dazzling whiteness by workmen of his grace. I thought then, in the long ago, that skins of a young doe bind fast and hard and bite with an unseeming haste and strange delight into my flesh as yet unused to being bound so tight.

But now I know that skins of a doe bind loosely in comparison with the incomprehensible, unfathomable, unsearchable ways of God. They take me, bound already in the skins of the young doe, and lift me up and nail me down onto the cross of the will and ways of God for me from that instant unto eternity.

It is thus bound and nailed, and only thus, that I, in the perfection of charity, can become pliant as his instrument. There is no other way for me. From henceforward I walk by being nailed to Christ's own will that is revealed to me through his priest.

From hence I cease to be as an entity. For out of flaming love I have surrendered utterly all of me into the hands of God stretched out to me. I have no will but his. My life is holocaust, complete. I must cease to be, then Christ in all his might will live in me.

Then I shall be a chalice, wrought of gold, that will exist but to assuage his thirst: I have no other destiny but this. But where I become a chalice of gold I must first be purified, in seven fires, from all the dross in me. The priest will make the fires. The priest will put me in until I am all clean and ready to be shaped, as God desires, into a chalice of love and fire.

The priest will fashion me without false pity, and I shall know the school of pain that is the school of saints. From hence my life must be living on his tree. For me, hunger and cold and whip and lash and hard, hard surfaces for sleep, so that I may learn the lesson of love's ecstasy.

These easy ways that will become more easy as I go along are but a start to teach my heart to grow, to expand, and take standing up what it must take to become a heart of utter love.

The priest will know what goes into the making of such a heart. In utter love of God and soul he must, he will, lead me up, up the path of outward pain and such, and then lead me up, up again, to learn to walk the peaks of death, nay, of annihilation of my own living self.

For this he will be watchful like the hawk, and be my hidden whip and cord that will lash me mercilessly in the full mercy of the Lord, watching for the slightest shadow on the transparency that must be me. For I am called to reflect in my gold Christ's face *perfectly*.

I know today that I am called to a slow martyrdom of growth in love, so as to be ready for the martyrdom of blood. Amen. Amen.

I Walk In His Light   *January 28, 1953*

Today my heart and I walk in his light. It shines like a strange, moving finger on all the shadows that we knew not we had, my heart and I. And the shadows vanish at his touch, and we are bathed in his light, and lighted up, my heart and I. A flame, ready to dance its flaming way into the souls of men.

Today we walk, my heart and I, in his immense and infinite strength that strengthens us through and through. Behold, we were so small, my heart and I, and now we are giants of his grace and know that we could do all things in him who strengthens us.

Today, my heart and I see clearly, and far, the holy words that men wrote (because the Crimson Dove touched them with its wings). These words leap up at us, and give us their kiss, and we become wise with the wisdom of simplicity.

Today my heart and I walk in the splendor of love. We feel that it draws us unto itself and then sends us out into the world of men, strong with its eternal, flaming strength. And then, it draws us in again, and we become a rhythm, a song of love, and love is God.

We walk in trust today, my heart and I. It has taken us up beyond the sky and there poured into us its tenderness, its might, and sent us back to earth in sheer delight. We rest now in its peace and know that we are immovable, like the Rock from which trust springs.

We entered today the domain of Lady Obedience, my heart and I, and found it vast, but knew that we are heir to its immensity. We cannot enter infinity without learning all its boundaries. We must come before the face of love in the full perfection of maturity.

Today, my heart and I are at rest on Christ's breast.

Peaks   *February 3, 1953*

Unto a strange, dark peak, our path leads us today, my heart and me. We are like two set apart from all the rest of living souls.

We walk all upwards. Slow is our step. Somehow it seems reluctant; yet it cannot be. For our Love bids us to walk that path and so in love we do. Yet our step is slow.

The path is strange. It winds and turns and turns again in such sharp, steep, and endless bends that we feel lost at times, my heart and I. For it appears there is no path behind the next turn or bend, and we will fall into the void that spreads so vast, so endless, right by our trembling feet.

And now my heart and I struggle in truth, for the path unto the peak that we must reach is more than steep. It is almost straight, up, up, up the face of a huge rock.

Just as we brace ourselves to climb, a wind comes from nowhere and tears us up, it seems, into a thousand shreds of pain. Yet we are voiceless, my heart and I, in our endless multiple pain.

And now we know the twisting path, and now we ken the thousand bends, and now we see why the sheer cliff; for this is how one enters in the light-dark land of utter loneliness our Love knew so well while he walked the earth.

We are all ready, Lord, my heart and I, to climb, to pant, to twist and turn, if it be your most holy will that we enter your loneliness; for we are lonely too for many things, but most of all for you.

"I am the Lord, your God, your Lover too. I know your loneliness and I alone will lead you into mine. I am the wind of great desire that fills you up with flame and fire.

"I steep you in my loneliness to send you out into worldliness that sears and kills so many, so many souls. Give them my pain, show them my sorrow; both you will learn.

"When you will reach the peak of my loneliness, be still, be pliant to my will and my desire. I want of you obedience, surrender so complete that you are not—I am in you. Then, a flame, you will descend, a feather crimson red, into the depths of souls, and there wrestle and conquer the worldliness that stifles them and makes my loneliness so utter, so complete.

"You are my nothingness. You are my emptiness. I wish it so, because then I can fill them both with me. But as yet you are not utterly obedient and your surrender is not complete. Descend in depth and then come back and hand to me all that is speck and dust of perfect obedience.

"And I will blow the dust and specks away and there will be your utter obedience, your perfect surrender, and I will make them and you my instruments of love. Amen. Amen."

Waiting   *February 4, 1953*

Alone, my heart and I are lying still in the still night, waiting, waiting we know not for what or whom.

There is great fear in us tonight. My heart and I are trembling all the while. We lie so still in this dark night.

We were immersed, my heart and I, in so much noise today that we cannot find a silent place to lie in this dark night.

It seemed to us all day that men's tongues were puppets pulled by unseen hands to clack and clack and make the noise around and about us to silence us.

But we went on against all noise with our song of love and pain and love again. We did not fail to speak of him who bade us speak or sing of him who is himself the Song of songs.

But now that we, my heart and I, are all alone in the dark night, we are afraid of their words that make such noise all around and about us. And so we lie still as can be, yet trembling all the while.

It seems to us our Love is gone and left us all alone in this dark night. And yet we know, my heart and I, it is not so. And then we lie and wait and try to think of days and nights that were when he was close and all was light and deep repose and all delight. And our thoughts make this dark night bright.

And yet we are afraid. Help us, oh Love, to conquer fear and lie still, still, in all the nights, dark or light, you will for us.

Waiting For My Love   *February 5, 1953*

We live, my heart and I, strangely these days, as if we faced two ways and yet walked but one.

There is about us, my heart and me, a wall of radiant floating mist that keeps us in and holds us in a garden all enclosed where we are still and waiting, waiting for our Love to enter and dwell within.

And yet, behold my heart and I are out there amongst the throngs, the noise, the market place, witnessing in words and deeds, as our Love commands, to his immense and infinite desire of all the souls that pass us by.

We live, my heart and I, strangely these days, as if we faced two ways yet walked but one.

We burn with desire of solitude and silence in our love; and yet we run, we leap into the crowds, the noise, because of him who is our Love.

We are a contradiction to ourselves, my heart and I. For we are so full of pain, so lonely, so bereft of all we love; and yet we are so sure, so straight about everything that we must do and be for our Love.

We are so strange these days, my heart and I. We see so strangely deep into men's hearts today that we are slow of speech, yet sure of what to say.

We feel so much, my heart and I, the pain, the tears, the pricks, the shame our Love must bear, that we are covered with them all and yet walk straight.

Time stands still for us these days; yet days go by so fast.

We cry at night, my heart and I, yet through the day we smile and laugh. Like mirrors might reflect the light, so do we reflect his love.

We Face Alone   *February 6, 1953*

We face alone, my heart and I, from the height of his throne and in the blinding light of his revealing, the heart of Lucifer and his designs against the Son of God who became man.

At our feet, before our eyes, the whole of it lies flat and clear and terrible in its entity of sheer intelligence directed by intense hate.

We see and tremble, it seems, until we faint, and faint not with fear; for what afrights us is not the hate nor its child, the plan of hate. We are afrighted, my heart and I, before the sight of man's free will. For there it stands in beauty unsurpassed, straight like the sword made by God's hands, shining like light that comes from him, guided by reason, flooded with faith, that both are lights infinitely supreme, that both are gifts of him who is and was and ever shall be, the uncreated perfection of Love triune.

Against this will, against its strength, against this reason that reflects intelligence supreme in facets small, against the blinding, singing, healing gift of faith, the bleak, cold darkness, dank, fetid, of hate moves in the slow, undulant way snakes have of moving noiselessly.

It cringes, it crawls in the thousand roads of human minds. It is so small at first, just like the mist, and then it stands up straight and gets quite thick. And then it pounces, strikes, devours men's faith, men's minds, men's wills, and moves again, slow, small, and still as death must be in mortal sin.

It stinks like it and brings with it utter decay. And yet, it does not strike as one would think. Like a windmill of hate, it strikes now here, now there, with the precision of a mind that is the incarnation of the opposite of light, of love, of God; and is permitted to challenge the free and beautiful will of man so that he can be freer to love and go into the heart of love with giant strides by freely melting his free will with God's.

My heart and I die, faint, revive, to die and faint and live again, before this sight of grace and hate fighting for the free will of man.

Behold the scheme, the plan of hate that Satan

spawned of late. Into the heart of men's closest reflection
of divine love, into the home where man is Christ, his
mate the Church, Satan moves with his most delectable
fruit, that seem to woman and man to be so sweet.

He offers them the kingdom of utter greed, clothed in
the vivid clothing of pride supreme that will, he says,
make them like gods of all they survey, and make them
kings of all they wish in flesh and goods and gold and
pomp.

The price of this is small indeed; or so he says. Just
dethrone obedience to him who died obedient unto death
for love of them.

It was, he says, a foolish thing to do in the first place;
and men of 1953 must realize obedience is obsolete. It
leads to slavery of will that no one with any sense in 1953
would need; for it would lead them all into a padded cell.

My heart and I die a thousand deaths, yet we live
again, as we behold attack upon attack upon the little
church of God, the home.

And then behold again the wounds that each of these
inflicts upon the whole of Christ's Body as it falls under
the fetid wiles of him whose breath is death.

For this my heart and I have been shaped. For now we
know we must descend from his throne into the thick of
this battle and stand alone in no man's land and hold on
high the light of him who shaped us well and is our all.

We know that we shall be and are torn into shreds of
flesh. But he who is Lord of all life will put us back together again, to stand and hold his light on high in no
man's land again, again. Amen. Amen.

Battered and Bruised   *February 9, 1953*

My heart and I have lost all light. We lie battered and
bruised and full of pain, somewhere where hate that
lashed at us today left us to die.

We saw our Love die before our eyes. We saw the nails of prejudice hit by the hammer of bleak hate nail his hands and feet. We stood by. We did not weep, because our tears were heavy stones upon our soul!

My heart and I have lost our light. We lay battered and bruised where hate left us lie when we saw our Love die. How strange, how strange that we keep on walking and talking amongst men when we know we are truly bruised and battered, stoned for Love's sake.

We cannot pray; there is no time. And yet prayer is our house. We journey forth, yet live within. Behold us in the midst of noise and din, standing in our house of prayer.

Look. See. It can be done by all who love Love crucified. They must remain by his side. I go away to do his work. They are a house divided yet made whole at the same time.

Woman Clothed In Silence   *February 10, 1953*

Up, up, into the blinding light, into the golden light, into the warm light that is no light at all, but love. I see the woman clothed in silence, ascend, ascend, and melt with love, becoming light herself.

Then she descends, herself a flame, and lying on her heart the Crimson Dove rests.

In the transparency of her eternal womb, a tabernacle of love supreme, lies her son who is the Son of God.

Above her head, invisible yet substantial, all powerful in benignity and infinite creative paternity, God, Father, bends.

And so, imprisoned in my thought, she is the Woman more terrible indeed than an army arrayed in battle; for at her feet prostrated, unable to behold such splendor, angels lie like fleecy clouds; infinite, adoring spirits of truth lying prone before the triune God in her.

Slender, young, small, she is now clothed in immensity, infinity, that is eternity. Maria!

Below, the depths of hell shiver, shudder, are rent with hate. Lucifer opens his wings of bleak, dead black, and cringes, yet rises in hate, his shadow on the earth where *she* shed light.

Betwixt them man stands alone, strong in her light, weak in his shadow. Light, darkness, face each other across the sword of man's free will. She holds in her hands a chalice pure. Graces flow in steady stream, blinding in beauty, strength, cascades of mercy and of love.

She holds in her hands a chalice pure. The Crimson Dove rests on her breast; the child lies in her womb; God, Father, pours his love on them. A sun shines above, around, beside her, and casts its light upon man below.

Satan—it is permitted so—stands over man, aside somehow, and hate and pride comes forth from him, a shadow bleak, a shadow deep, that falls on man below.

And now my heart and I, in thought, stand by and see the Woman and the serpent fight for the soul of man who stands alone betwixt the two.

Now all is gone. We stand alone, my heart and I, encircled, bound by men hurrying to and fro. There is no woman, the serpent cannot be seen, but souls of men are now revealed. And we, my heart and I, are sent therein somehow to fight the fight of light.

Maria! Mother! Virgin! Bride of the Most High! Help us, my heart and me, to do the will of him who is your Love and your Son; so that we be filled with his grace through our cupped hands and unafraid of him whom we must fight because your Love, which is ours too, bids us to fight with all his might.

One waits upon this fight of light of love and dark of hate.

Oh man, who stand and hold free will, free gift of God, passport of your charity, arise, arise and choose your side. Take her, Virgin, Mother, Bride of light. Drink deep from the chalice of her hands and slay Satan with the sword of your free will.

Come, arise. I am the voice of light, I who like you am but man, creature of Father and Son and Crimson Dove, triune Love. Their nothingness and emptiness sent to fill your soul with their might, because grace comes free to them through her and then to man to feed the souls of other men. And grace is light, and light goes through emptiness, nothingness, and becomes visible from like to like. Oh listen, soul, to my weak voice, and hear in it the thunder of God's will for you.

But souls are deep and men are weak. They hurry by. Their eyes are sealed to all the things my heart and I stammer so childishly to them.

She stands alone upon her throne of love and light. The Crimson Dove upon her breast, the Child within her Virgin's womb, God, Father, bends in love on her.

But darkness grows from hell on men. She weeps, her tears are bittersweet. And angels stop their song of joy and stand aghast at Mary's tears.

But men pass by intent on gold and lust, power and pomp. And the Crimson Dove lifts up its head. The Son arises, bleeding to death. Above the two, yet one with them, God, Father, rises up in wrath; and still unseen but felt in all this terrible, awesome night, makes ready to strike men dead.

But the Woman's face, all wet with tears, looks up and stays his justice clear of men. And they live on again to make their choice once more between the light of love and the dark of hate.

My heart and I are as one dead before the sight of our thought. Oh Maria!

Crumbling, Cracking   *February 11, 1953*

Crumbling, cracking, leaking, creaking, the walls of souls, the walls of minds are in chaos, in turmoil, beneath the wind and storm of hell.

Alone Love walks amidst the stones; alone Love stands amidst the ruins; still loving, ready, able to restore all things to their tranquility of order, should but the souls, the minds cry out and beg to drink of his wine divine. But souls and minds are numb or dead beneath the weight of raping hands and shadows bleak.

They scream, they rush, they die, are squashed, because they take no time to seek the wine of love divine. The screaming hordes rush endless by, dying of thirst whilst wine divine is standing by, filled to the brim with healing draught.

My heart and I have drunk the wine and we are full and safe from any rape, from all the weight of bleak and frantic hate. But we are sad beyond all sadness. There are in us tears that weigh us down, stone upon stone—a stony crown.

For we behold our Love standing alone and no one stopping to drink his wine of love. And we remember so many things. The wine we drank filled to the brim our small capacity. We overflow with love and pity. And yet, though we descend into the depth of men's hearts and souls, we cannot give a drop of wine unless they ask. Free will is such that even God cannot do violence to it.

House of Love   *February 13, 1953*
                                     Sacred Heart Convent

We entered into the house of love, the meeting place of love and peace, my heart and I. We are complete—love, peace, and I.

Yet we abide in a strange wind that seemed to have been waiting for us to come, my heart and me. It came like storm, like flashes of blinding light, as if glory must embrace the night souls dwell in, in expectation of love's caress.

It came and lifted us from inside us, and lifted us alone of soul unto some yet untrodden height. And there we saw love and the foe fight for the souls of men.

The sight of such a might made us like death. But a touch of light made us alive again. On such a height it seems a soul lives betwixt and between what men call death and God calls life.

We saw the foe attack in serried ranks millions of souls at the same time. We saw free will within those souls bend, sway and break, or stand straight and still.

And then—oh sight beyond all seeing—we saw *the light* shed its might, a flow of graces that looked like facets, gems, of the Light itself. Iridescent, incandescent flames imprisoned in a thousand settings of Love's begging. Cascading down from heights unknown, incomprehensible, inaccessible, unfathomable, unreachable, all converging into the hands of her alone. Encompassed, reached, fathomed, comprehended, the Source which she bore in her virginal womb.

Cupped hands, she stood above the high height of us, silent, immense, yet slight. In an unceasing stream graces poured into her hands that made a chalice strangely big, for they were small.

Eye could not see the rush, the flow of graces from above to below, that filled the chalice of her hands and spilled, cascaded, resplendent upon men's souls.

And then—oh miracle of love—the broken were made whole, the bent straight, the bruised all healed, the strong, the still became stronger, stiller, almost perfect.

Then again the foe attacked. We stood and trembled, swooned, died, lived again.

But now we know what happens to the souls of men on earth. We saw, because the wind of love lifted us to heights above. Amen. Amen.

Love Supreme *February 13, 1953*

Light incandescent, light that is God, unseen, unfelt, apprehended without apprehending. Bending without moving, to emptiness and nothingness. Lost in the midst of earth and sea of what men call "the world."

Whence is this to me who is as if I were not, yet am? Behold the utter emptiness that in truth I am. Filled with longing that seems slighter than the cry of a baby. Filled with hunger that seems in itself no hunger at all. Filled with fire that seems colder than ice.

Light incandescent, light that is God, unseen, unfelt, apprehended without apprehending, reposing in your own splendor, surpassing comprehension of angels! Loving with love triune in One. Father to Son begetting the Crimson Dove of love. Stillness that is all movement, movement that is all stillness. Creative in both beholding each other—sufficient, complete, uncreated, supreme. What can you find in a soul like mine, so supine, so earthbound, so filled with the sounds of death! Heavy with nothing, pregnant with sloth. What can attract Love Uncreated to such!

Triune, Uncreated, Supreme, Father and Son, Crimson Dove between. Three in One, One in Three. Fruitful, creative in motion that is Love Uncreated—Triune and thy God. In creative love conceived the soul to our image and likeness, with love supreme. Loose particle, divine flame, set burning in a piece of clay to the shape of a man!

Love Uncreated sent its creation to bring its fecundity to rest in itself. Love over-flowing, Love un-apprehended, desired to be loved by facets of itself into eternity. Souls are the facets; souls are the feathers that float from the wings of the Dove that is crimson, the Love of Father and Son. Feathers that descend for an instant called time, meant to ascend and return to whence they came! Feathers that should sing as they float, of the love whence they came, of the love whence they go.

Emptiness, yes, to be filled to the brim with the love of the Three that are but One—Triune. Nothingness, yes, to be shaped by God into intellect that will chant the glory of him who has set it on the sword of a will free as the wind, and placed in it, like a bird in a nest, the free gift of faith to illuminate both and to render to God the chant of the Gloria and the service of love. This love, though lifted above, is turned to the neighbor it sees and in whom it beholds, with the eyes of faith, Love Supreme, Triune, creative self-sufficiency, fecund movement that never ceases! Yet seems to stand still because no one anywhere in the spheres can apprehend the movement of love of Father, Son, and Crimson Dove.

Flames of the all-creative Flame triune, that souls are meant to free themselves from, ought then to re-enter God from whence they came. Burning lights to bring with them other flames to render glory to the uncreated Fire of Love Supreme!

Dark Night *February 19, 1953*

The night was dark, and so was I. For we, my heart and I, went in the dark, what dark we cannot tell. We never went in that dark before.

It was a dark where mirrors stood and shone so bright as if they were the light they were not.

We did not want to look in them. But no matter how we closed our eyes, my heart and I, we saw ourselves reflected there from every side.

It was not our earthly eyes that saw, nor were they the eyes of our soul. They were the eyes of strangers, yet we knew they were our eyes too.

We saw ourselves as we appear to others—or so it seemed. And what we saw was far from fair.

We saw a face that showed the wear, the tear of time, and spoke to us with sneering grace of our youth that passed us by. We saw our body as it looked, in truth, a sight so sad that we should have dissolved in tears.

And then we saw our soul and heart bear all the marks of sin and earthly dust. We saw it wounded and healed with ugly scabs and ugly scars; and it was shown to us in full how old, how ugly, was the outside and inside of us.

And yet we were not at all disturbed, my heart and I. We got somehow the strength to look and see in truth what we looked like. We shed no tears. We did not care. Somehow we stood just looking there.

It did not matter, for we were what love and life had made us be. So all we did was lift our ugly wounds, our scabs and scars and tired flesh, to him who made it and to whom we had but this and love to give.

And as we lifted the whole of us such as it was, the darkness vanished, and we were left to bathe in light and peace that said for us to rest.

"This is well, woman from a strange land my Mother loves and so do I, that you saw what you look like to those whose eyes are sealed and held.

"I want it thus because I wish you to be grounded in the twelve degrees of humility. Oh, I have given you simplicity, but this does not preclude your growth in my humility. I want you humble, humble unto the dust you came from. I want you humble.

"And then I want so very much that you should know in full my perfect virtue—trust in me for everything unto eternity. This is my wish.

"Abandonment must come with it, for only love can know the fullness of it.

"You must be detached from all except my will. You understand, do you?

"Humility, trust, abandonment, detachment, each flowering in you, my garden enclosed. You need so much of each to flower well before I come and take my rest in you.

"For don't you see, you who are so small in virtue and so slow to know and understand, how I delight in using your nothingness, your emptiness. For you are naught, and empty too, and almost ready to be filled with me.

And I abide in all these virtues that come from me and lead a soul to the perfection of my charity.

"I make clear again, again. I want you shaped; for you can be so fair, so fair to me. Amen. Amen."

The Wind   *February 21, 1953*
                                                New London, CT

The wind, the wind roared, tore, twisted and broke all things it touched. It wreaked its vengeance on my soul and tried to break through all its walls.

The storm, the rain were lashed by wind into an elemental tidal wave that howled its triumphant song each time it broke a tree or wrecked a roof. It danced, it danced the dance of madness like the lunatic that it was.

It took all of my obedience to stand and face the storm alone.

I knew that it was more than wind, than rain, than sleet. I knew it was Satan's rage hurled at me, because at every turn I botched and frustrated his plans in souls. But there again, it was not I; for I was but a pebble small in the palm of my Love's hand.

"Let go and leave the wind alone. No storm can touch you when I say so. For winds and waves obey my words. Rest now, because soon you walk up a hill called Calvary with me.

"For years you made the way with me. And now I shall make it with you. One by one we shall descend into the well of all these stations you have loved so much and which each have become, unknown to you, a part of you.

"Descend, descend into the sea of pain that encompassed me. Stand still. Behold my Gethsemani. And then feel Judas's kiss touch my fair skin and see it blanch from pain within me.

"Behold the throngs, the soldiers strong hacking me to death and misery. And then behold Pilate and see how fastidious a Roman can be. He knew my innocence and yet condemned me, but in perfumed waters washed his hands. Yet who would wash his heart?

"Behold and see perfect justice condemned imperfectly. Do you begin to understand what was meant by this first station of my passion of love for you?

"Look back. Look forward. For you I will open the rest of time. See how injustice abounds on earth and how charity lies wounded unto death.

"It had to be this way. There was no other to expiate the sins of a million years and a thousand billion men who did and do and will continue to wound charity because they kill without mercy her daughter justice, through fear, human respect, love of themselves or gold.

"I am *Caritas* your God. How else could I atone for this dark sin that brought my Father's anger, except by becoming the exemplar of such a verdict, of such a pain? Because, you see, Pilate, by condemning me, gave me the way to repair for love's wounds and those of justice, and thus give strength to all who bear injustice in the evils of the earth.

"It is because I knew of this that I spoke to men of justice fair and told that they who hunger for it shall be filled.

"You see, I'll fill them; for I hungered for justice, being pure justice myself. But I met injustice, and touching me it became a flame. Men have burned with it joyfully for my sake. I bore it with a song for your sake.

"Thus I opened the gates of love by standing before Pilate, my love."

Travellers   *February 22, 1953*

My heart and I, we are tonight two travellers fallen by the wayside. It seems the load is now beyond our strength and we are drenched in sweat as we lie there covered with dust and biting at gritty sand.

We are laid low by the weight of a cross. We are laid low by a thousand blows. Streams of blood flow unseen from a thousand wounds that cannot be seen.

The wind is like a beast unchained. It lashes us again and again. Now will it lash us to bits? How long will it whip us to death?

We are so weary, my heart and I. We are too weary to live or die. We only can lie here and bite the dust.

Catharina Mea   *February 23, 1953*

Oh, Love, Beloved. Forgive, forgive my speech that breaks into yours. Forgive my foolish heart these words of yours, these words of mine, these words that come so strangely from what men call "outside," "nowhere," and that exist only in thoughts that I do not think. And so they are truly yours, checked and re-checked in deep obedience. You do not wish them to be read by others except the eyes of thy priest. Oh, Love, say that you don't, and saying it, forgive the simplicity of your foolish child!

"Catharina mea, there is nothing to forgive, foolish heart. Brides speak to their loves at all times, and souls can speak, must speak, to the God that loved them enough to die, when they wish, which should be always. No one listens better to words of petition, love, and contrition than I, Love Incarnate. No one can know as well as I the depth of tears, nor dry them up as fast as I.

"So weep, and speak, beloved of mine, without fear, and in all love. But listen too, and hear well the words of him who is *the Word*, thy God and Lover supreme, and then obey, obey, obey.

"Now I repeat, write. Because the words are mine, so are the thoughts, for I have permitted thee to undergo trials at the hand of the foe; and these to record for others to read.

"For it is I who wished that you write *Journey Inward*,

only this time you are the hand and I the mind. For journeys are made by souls whom I guide to myself in my own way. And they, so small, so empty, so slow of mind and foolish of heart, would be long lost on their journeys inward was I not there to guide and lead.

"And so, Catharina mea, you write, but only what I permit to be written. None of it is yours. I desire to leave to my priest, all of it, to do what he wishes with it, because this is part of the night you must be in. This is part of the utter surrender that I desire from you.

"Nothing must concern you, foolish heart that loves well. All is mine, and if I wish that others see and doubt and scoff, that is the whip that I can lay upon your back as once was laid a whip upon my own. Comprehend, understand my command. I want you to have no other will than mine. All of you belongs to me, and you shall come unto my throne *my way*. *That* is your journey inward. When it is finished, then I shall behold myself in thee, and you will be all absorbed in Me.

"And so, this is my wish, that you give these written leaves to my priest, and then annihilate all thoughts of them in thy memory until I bring them back to thee piecemeal, or whole, as it pleases Me. You are emptiness, being made ready for fruitful fecundity by Me through my priest, who will, at my command, empty first all the dust of worldliness, and then fill thee with, and give thee over to, Marie, to give to me.

"Oh, Catharina mea, I am a tremendously impatient Lover. Hasten, hasten to obey and be pliant to my desire in utter emptiness and nothingness. Then you shall bring to Me, through my fecundity, souls, souls. I thirst for them, I thirst for them. Hasten, hasten to die to self utterly, utterly, Catharina mea. I thirst! Sitio!"

Spiritual Direction   *February 28, 1953*

"Outwardly you will just do what you are told by him,

step by step, and nothing more. You will live not by the
day nor the hour but by the minute, the second of it; and
do all the things that come in them hidden away in Combermere.

"It is I who will make it what I want to make of it, and
in doing so, I will show you the secrets of the black heart
that you must understand in order to fight the wiles of
hell.

"But now listen well, child of my heart. You must re-
port this to my priest with the greatest of care.

"He is to teach you the heavy discipline of leaving all to
me, in the duty of the day, the hour, and all that goes into
making it. That duty should be prompt, so prompt that it
will make your will my steel. And this means now, when
you are back in Combermere.

"I want you mortified outside, inside, so that you are a
tool as pliant as a sapling in spring. He may, he can, use
any means he wishes; for the Crimson Dove will tell him
all he needs to know.

"But this I want clear, crystal clear. He must understand, without a shadow of a doubt, that gardeners of my
garden enclosed may take delight in it; but also must go
and work in it with shears and knife, and cut and prune
to make its beauty delight my eye.

"I want it clear that if he fails to cut one tiny shoot that
may offend my sight, he will have deeply wounded my
heart.

"And now write down again that I want you more obedient than you are, because you see, child of my love,
your obedience is not for you alone. I use it to dethrone
the foe and stop his incarnate pride to rob me of the heart
of my bride—its priests.

"He is a priest himself, and if he cuts and prunes and
makes you what I want, obedience incarnate to me, then
he is working to restore the heart of my bride to me.

"And now, listen well. I said to you that he will lead
souls to me through her who loves him much. But let it be
clearly understood; the way will be of utter obedience,

stability, mortification, annihilation of self, trust, accept-
ance and *caritas*.

"If and when I will send him another garden enclosed
to be gardener in, I will ask the Crimson Dove to make
clear the 'where,' the 'how,' and the rest of it.

"Just now you are unique inasmuch as you have become a garden enclosed. I have made it so myself and
have sent many priests to labor in it. And now he is master of it until I come myself to dwell in it.

"There are two more that are being shaped now with
enclosures. But the rest are grown to plow and to seed
with obedience, stability, mortification, annihilation of
self; nothing more.

"Let that be understood clearly. For Combermere is my
novitiate of love for souls to be used in the fighting of the
doom that is nigh. And I can fight only with the instrumentality of utter obedience, stability, death to self. Understand this, and tell my priest.

"And now, write well. For he must understand once
and for all that now is the time—I say *now*—to begin that
shaping of you. For soon he will go, and only I know
when he will come back to be the master of the souls and
house of Combermere.

"You must be trained before he goes to the plan and the
road and the ways I have spoken so much about, because
only then can you begin to understand the secrets of Beel-
zebub.

"I have spoken. Be it done according to my word.
Amen. Amen."

Dark and Light   *March 7, 1953*

The night is dark, the night is light. For my heart and I
abide in the heart of the night and contemplate the Light.
Oh! Love of mine! What is a night, what is the dark when
it will lead my heart and me into the light of your caress,

into the ecstasy of your embrace!

"Woman of the strange land my mother loves, and so do I. You do not know what mystery is hidden in your land. And you, O Land, immense in height, in depth, you stand aloof, alone. You dream dreams of caritas, justice, redress on the knees of hope that springs like water from its loving breast.

"Your land is holy. Yes, indeed. For it has been hanging on the tree with me for centuries. With its noble head upon my breast, it went on through tears and pain, dreaming its eternal dream in me, its triune God.

"It knows that taste of my cup. It is even now drinking its last drop. It knows how torn flesh feels, each bit of it. It knows the salty taste of tears, each drop of it. It knows the dust of a million roads, the choking, dry smell of each. For it has lain, as I have lain, drained on each of them.

"It knows the strange and lancing pains of every knob of every grain that a lacerated back can feel while nailed to the tree, each one of it. The crown rests deep on its aching head, as deep in parts as it encompassed mine.

"And you are the child of this vast and holy land, its dreams are seeded deep into your heart. Its mystery of suffering is in your eyes, reflected like its changing skies.

"My mother came to Fatima to plead again with the children of men (she loves her very own so much) to atone and pray so that they may begin to love me back. For if they don't, then the foe will eat them up. She asked that Russia should be brought back to the man in white, for that is all it needs to make my tree its bridal bed, and be one completely with me.

"My mother came in 1917 and you were just seventeen yourself. You did not know (your eyes were held) that this was the day that the ray of Fatima touched your heart. For Father, Son, and Holy Ghost decided then that you would be a grain of Holy Russia (with its mystic soul, its dreamer's mind, its heart so full of love of us) lifted up by our wind to bring all of it to the world at large.

Caritas   *March 18, 1953*

My heart and I went to a dance last night. It seems we
left the earth, or were we still there? We stood and
watched a dance of stars that made us—my heart and
me—so full of joy that it seemed we joined in and danced
with all the stars, our dance of joy.

It did not matter where we looked, or what star was
there before our eyes. They were all dancing in a gracious,
scintillating, dazzling way. And yet it seemed that their
dance was one of unalloyed joy because it was not a dance
at all but a song in motion. A welcome song for One who
was a brighter, bigger, lighter star than any in the firma-
ment.

Slow, sure. At first the stars danced on to music steady,
profound in tune. But then, quite suddenly, they danced
wildly, as if drunk with joy, to music fast, melodious, that
made my heart and me swoon with the joy of it.

One star stood out—right out of the moon that was herself moving to the tune. *That* star trembled with joy so
much that it could dance only by standing still! Its move-
ments were in tune, but full of awe and unbearable expectation that made it grow in size and elation.

And suddenly, all the stars went mad with joy and
drunk with music that seemed to be the echo of God's
voice, or the reflection of his smile.

For there, on the one star that was so full of love and
languidness, stood, bright as the sun outshining the
moon, "Our Lady of the Dancing Star," Mediatrix of all
graces. As if unable to bear the weight of so much beauty,
the star dipped, sank, came up again, and then began to
tremble with love.

Amid the dancing stars and the dipping moon surrounded with a soft white light, the Lady of the dancing
stars stood, clothed in gold, over Combermere. Her hands
were so full of light that it seemed the night faded away in
sheer delight, and went to sleep at her gold-shodden feet.

My heart and I stood still. For joy held us so tight we could not breath. The Lady of the dancing star, Mary Mediatrix, bent over Combermere, and lifting her hands, let their blinding rays fall on the village of Combermere, her house. Yet, they seemed to spread, fanwise, across the earth, which suddenly became itself a dancing star.

Yes, my heart and I went to a dance last night.

Peace and Pain   *March 21, 1953*

My heart and I think thoughts of peace and love today, all passion flecked.

There is about us a stillness deep, and a strange pain that comes and goes like snow in spring now thaws, now freezes, only to thaw and run again with a glad refrain down a thousand hills into the bosom of a river blue—or is it of a scarlet heart?

We do not quite know, because the thoughts of love fill us so full that we cannot think quite clearly even of peace. Yet we know that peace is here and that we walk in it.

Yet, strange (or is it?) pain still holds us in its domain so vast that it seems we always will live in some part of it.

We do not mind, my heart and I, because today we somehow know that love and pain are one and the same; because, in truth, love's domain is but a tree, and love hangs from it—a bunch of grapes so sweet that we feel that if we eat too much of them death will claim my heart and me.

For love meets pain, and then the two become one that takes us up in ecstasy that must, we think, be the end of us. And yet, somehow we live and breathe and even manage to walk amongst the sons of men inebriated as we are with love.

Today our Love met us on the way and spoke to us so gently; yet we knew that he meant what he said in the fullness of his truth.

"Beloved, this is the time to enter a lonely road, the road of being all mine, inside and out.

"Here is the gate of it—holy indifference. Come, enter in, and leave behind all created things, all understanding. It is so short a word, yet 'all' means just what it says—all.

"Henceforth you are all mine, walking to me on the lonely road of eternity that is all dark in faith without any light but me, content to be alone, content when I lift you upon my throne, content when I throw you to the foe to battle for souls, or just to see you fight his pride and lay it low, so that he may take time to simmer down, and in that time my grace will work on souls and bring them back to me, because you fought the foe for love of me."

Good Friday   *April 3, 1953*

The touch was feathery, the pain a fire burning fiercely and suddenly, like dry wood ignited by a living, hot and burning coal.

Dissolution, annihilation, became absolution to one in the throes of death. And yet, before annihilation was complete or dissolution did its deed, the whole was whole again and pain the queen of it.

From then the cycle became a song with its slow-moving rhythm. Now we dissolved, my heart and I. Now we were annihilated and now all whole again, in the embrace of Lady Pain. And then the whole rhythm started again.

We floated off on a sea of blood and then floated right back in again. Blood bathed us and left its sweet, strange taste on our lips. Its strange and fearsome smell filled us. And then taste, smell, receded back again where they came from; and someone touched us. Again the touch was feathery and yet the pain a burning fire.

And so it went and came and went again through the strange day of joy and death. We walked, we talked, we seemed to do all things we had to. And yet no one knew what all the time was happening to my heart and me.

The secrets of the King remain his secrets unrevealed. The hidden wounds on our feet were hidden still. The little open ones that came on our hands went by unnoticed by sealed eyes. The shoulders, back, the head, the face remained serene, their wounds unseen by those around and about us.

We walk in a pain today, my heart and I. And in the very heart of this love-day there is in us at one and the same time a rendezvous between life and death chaperoned by love. And muted but clearer as the hours slip by—as hours will—is the distant song of joy.

We walk in death. We burn like live coal. Pain stretches us on its marriage bed. Blood floats us out and floats us in and we are truly betwixt and between. And yet serenity fills us with peace, and love brings an unknown bliss, bitter as gall and vinegar, and yet when it touches our lips it is like choicest wine.

He cannot hold us tight. His hands are nailed. And yet we know today, my heart and I, that we lie on our marriage bed.

For his lips are his; and though cracked, dry, the kiss of his mouth is soft and sweet and sends my heart and me up into the darkening sky—high, high, so high that we can see the sun shine warm and bright, making ready to welcome the death of death tomorrow night.

The Trinity   *April 27, 1953*

Sea of infinity, sea of divinity, most holy, adorable, unique Trinity, beholds itself in a finite sea,

Created by the Father that has also infinity, meant body and soul to reflect the glory of the Three, meant one day to come back into the sea of infinity from which it descended,

The sea of the unique, most adorable Trinity in the perfect unity of love.

The Ties Are Cut   *May 10, 1953*

One by one, the ties are being cut. By whom? When? How? I do not know.

All that I know is that my heart and I slowly feel we are being cut off from all the things men value in themselves. We seem to float, yet behold, we walk the hard earth quite steadily.

Or then again it seems to us that we are a verdant field all strewn with dead. Behold there lies completely dead all interest in passing things. We look and look and wonder how it held our attention, our interest, for so long.

We read, but only that which should be read. The rest lies dead at our feet. And yet it seems but yesterday we read and read so many things.

Events come and events go, marching along the screen of time; shadows that leave but passing marks and for us are dead as nails. For now we know that they are but shadows and we are living in a substance that we know is neither a shadow nor a dream, but true, for it is God.

Possessions frighten us. Even now we behold their skeleton on the verdant green that is ourselves, a fertile field. We crave bare cells of soul and heart, whitewashed and clean, where God can rest at ease, it seems.

All ties of blood are cut clean too; but they are lifted up and lie in the very center of his heart. Now we know our heart loves all in his own heart.

Yet strange somehow there are still ties that bind us. They must be cut and that quickly too. And though we know he will do so, my heart and I fear the pain of this last cutting very much.

Now why is that?

So Many Roads   *May 11, 1953*

My heart and I are alright today.

There seemed to be so many roads to him, but we couldn't walk all the roads at the same time. So we turned round and round until from sheer weariness we could not see the way at all.

We got lost in some place that was roadless. Then we got confused, my heart and I, and very frightened. Lights came on that weren't lights at all. We prayed over them and they died. So we decided that we would stand still until he showed us the way, because it wouldn't do at all to follow lights that die when you pray.

But now we've found the way; we are alright, my heart and I.

It is very simple when you know. But it takes so long to see when you are tired, confused, and full of doubts. It is simple, as all you have to do is take the hardest road of all, for that is his road. We never thought of that until late today.

So behold us now, my heart and I, walking into a fog, undesirous to know what the next step brings. But we can feel so many things. The stones are knife-sharp under our feet and cut them deep; the branches of trees we can't see tear our back in a thousand shreds.

But we are not disturbed, my heart and I, for now we know it is the road he wants us to go.

All things have been taken away from us, my heart and me. We are imprisoned in a strange and walking cell that doesn't stop our ascent over stones as sharp as knives, yet encloses us like night. We are content to be that way if he desires us to be imprisoned this day.

In all this traveling we are not allowed to walk a step without a guide. Ours is strange. He seems to seek the sharpest stone, the lowest branch, the highest peak. He seems to be there to make the hardest road harder. He wants us to crawl on our knees, turn left or right.

One thing he never asks us is to go back. Outside of that, there seems to be no sense to his guiding us that way.

But we understand today, my heart and I. Our senses are taken away from us one by one. We asked to love the Sacred Heart so much as to become a slave, a thing, to a man's will that is God's. For our guide is no one else but Christ himself in the guise of this man who is his priest.

Now utterly subjected, imprisoned, walking a steep ascent in the domain of Lady Pain, we are content, my heart and I, for we have found the way which is his way.

All is well with us today, my heart and me.

Fatima Remembered   *May 13, 1953*

The curtain is still closed, but soon it will be pulled apart, and men will understand more the message of the Mother of God. Truly it is pitiful to see how sad she is, how full of tears. It is pitiful to see because they don't love Him as they should. It is pitiful to see. Do not be so sad, my Lady.

Behold the world. Behold the foe gleeful. He dances his macabre dance, his floor the souls of men. And then again it isn't, for suddenly they all arise and dance with him, his dance of lust, greed, selfishness—obscene. How ugly it all is! The light of God falls on this mob and it is thrown right back into His face.

There she stands, so sad, so sad, her hands filled with a million graces that could in an instant change the face of the whole earth. But they just look at them and throw them off and spit on them and go on dancing their dance with Satan, leading these unholy things.

There she stands, so sad, beholding all the graces trampled down. Drop by drop the graces come from His million wounds, and drop by drop they change into graces. He bleeds to death for love of them and they go on dancing their unholy dance and jeer at Him as He dies. And she stands by, so very sad, surrounded by a few who love.

But look, there and there, millions of them. What is pain when it is offered up? A drop against a sacrilege, blasphemy, monstrosity before my eyes, an orgy of man's soul gone mad—for that is what it is: men mad, split in two by him who is master of dividing and ruling. He offers them, oh silly fools, the will-o'-the-wisp, a fake, an unwholesome dream. He lures them with his lies and tantalizes them with shadows passing swift.

And there He hangs and bleeds for them. And there she stands beneath His cross, and looks and looks, and is so sad.

There is no story tonight. The picture is all that I have been told to tell tonight. That is all.

I Bleed For Love   *May 13, 1953*

"This is the picture of today. I hang and bleed for love. I, Love, am the fruit of the love tree and hang on it. One by one, my drops of blood fall down. Mary gathers up the drops into a chalice no one can see, given to her by my Father. And then she lifts it up to him and it atones. Cries out each drop: 'Caritas—love.' And I redeem. The movement is continual, from the day I hung on Calvary's gray hill, against the darkened sky, unto the end of time.

"It is true that I do not die again, on that one Calvary and that one cross; nor does she stand alive and brokenhearted beneath it, a statue of all sorrows men ever knew piercing her heart. No, that one act is done.

"But until the end of time, I bleed on a thousand Calvaries. For wherever men walk on this earth, there their God on a cross dies forevermore for them. I die in blacks, whites, reds, yellows; in all the races I die again a thousand deaths.

"They crucify me with the nails of complacency, greed, selfishness, and I die on crosses made of strange unknown woods. The cross of lust, pride, sloth, selfishness. I die in empty churches where no one cares whether I live or die—or so it seems. For no one pays any mind to the millions of poor who step inside.

"Wherever men walk the earth, there stands a cross and on it dies their God. Wherever I hang on the tree, my Mother stands beneath it with me.

"I love the souls of men so much that if it were needed I would go back and die again. But I am condemned, it seems, by the free will of men—that I gave them as a gift, that should be given back to me with joy—condemned to loneliness. My blood is shed, the treasure is in my Church. I am the way, she the gate. I wait in the heart of her who is my bride, wait to be loved back. No wonder she was sad.

"Behold, just as she said, the picture is quite true. But oh, the tragedy of it! To have shed my blood in vain; to love as passionately as only Love can love, and not be loved back. No wonder when I saw that, I sweated blood beneath the gnarled old olive trees of Gethsemani.

"Enter into that thought and see what my Father, I, and the Crimson Dove see—uncreated Love rejected, Love incarnate rejected. A mendicant at the door of a million hearts I created begging but one thing: to be loved in return. And millions laugh and jeer and don't want to deal with the divine ragman who is willing to take what no one would look at, the tatters of human love for him, crumbs. They who owe their very breath to me refuse this.

"You who pass by, would you give me the alms of your love? I am a beggar, not for any of the goods of this earth; I am a beggar for your love. Behold my hands and feet all open and my side all pierced. I am the King of pain. My head is covered with a crown that pierces every part of me, and I desire with a great desire to bleed for you; I desire to die for you.

"I am the beggar on the road of life that begs but for your love. Behold the angels falling down, adoring the Beggar. Behold the universe and spheres going around because I ordered. All nature, beasts, plants, and water are still at my command, and I stand at the crossroads of life and beg for your love, O soul of man.

"You who pass by, will you give me your heart? I died for it. I created it. And yet I stand at the crossroads of life and beg for your love. I, the Lord who holds your breath on his pierced palm, stand at the crossroads and beg your heart.

"And they pass by. And not even one listens to the voice of his own uncreated God, except maybe one or two that stop. But what of the rest?

"Now you understand why this is the century of mystics. So many have failed me that I must raise holocausts and victims, and men and women of low rank that know how to love, because the kingdom of those who don't is growing fast apace.

"Behold me standing at the crossroads with empty hands. How can I come before my Father with just the free will of men who turned away from me, their God? Some must be ready to atone for the hordes that pass me by without a glance, bent to go over to the foe. They can, you know.

"But I have weapons. Grace comes to men through men. There is the answer. Give me the souls that by their lives will show the face of love, my own. I'm tired of words.

"Give me the mirror of a soul that mirrors my face alone. You see what I mean when I speak of surfaces unruffled. They make the best mirrors of all. Give me mirrors clean that will mirror the face of love, my own.

"The domain of Lady Pain makes mirrors without blemish. Obedience polishes them, chastity frames them, poverty holds them up at the right height for all to see. And you, my priests, use these to make mirrors for me: Lady Pain, poverty, chastity and obedience. These belong to all baptized in my name, each according to his soul. You have been ordained to give them my grace and my truth as well as myself—sacrifice and food.

"With these and the rest, produce mirrors for me. For if you don't, the eyes of your soul will never mirror my own, for they will be lost in the darkness of hell where I abide not.

"True, I, your Lord of hosts, stand a beggar at the crossroads of life, a beggar for your love. But I demand of you who are myself, mirrors, that millions might mirror me. Otherwise, millions will die an eternal death and the rest will spend centuries in catacombs. There won't be any other place to go.

"I stand at the crossroads of life, a beggar for your love. Amen. Amen."

Mary Speaks   *May 15, 1953*

"In rest, your soul disposed, Catharina mea, there was no fault. It was permitted and it will bring quite many blessings that you don't suspect. Be at peace. All is well.

"I am the Lady of the stars, the dancing, joyous stars. I am the Lady of Combermere. You were quite right to call me that. For you see, the chapel will be to my Immaculate Conception, and men, women and children will call me quite familiarly Our Lady of Combermere. It won't be long now and my Son will live with you and all in this house. I shall be there with you.

"So you received permission, did you not today? We talked a little to our favorite son, the man in white, and those who sign for him. Don't worry much about financing the thing; when I decide to have a chapel, I finance it. Pray to me, you who are enchained in my loving slavery.

"I want to talk to you about my Son on this Friday. Who will console us? Who will wipe off our tears? Who will silently keep company with me under the cross? Who will love until he has become a burning flame and nothing else? Who?

"The tears of my Son are like a flood as he beholds the multitudes who aren't there. Who will come in their stead? His eyes are dim from pain and pain again, inflicted by the millions who live in mortal sin.

"Who is there to give their back, to take the rod, the whip, away from his? The sleepless night wears on and on. He is dragged from throne to throne, from room to room, from patio to patio, from Herod to Pilate. There is no rest for his weary body. Who will have unrest for him? Who will become a bed for him? To so become you must go on wood.

"Did he eat from Holy Thursday until he died? Who will fast and abstain for his sake? Console a Mother's heart. Go into the highways, byways, rural lanes and city streets, and find me souls willing to do that."

Catherine: I go.

"Come back. This is not the way I want you to find him. If I wanted souls like that I would speak to them as I did to you."

Catherine: You're asking me? You're asking me? Me? But of course!

"There is only one way that the world will be restored to my Son in whose glory I abide. There is only one way: for each soul to do her part who loves the Lord of my heart. For the time is past for mediocrity. The time is past for half measures. The foe has waxed strong. His growth is almost complete. And now I come to beseech soul by soul to repair by the two arms of prayer and mortification."

The Evil Suffocates Me   *May 17, 1953*

The evil suffocates me at times, my heart and me. We have been living in it these last days. It hates us. We are so watchful, and yet it sneaks past us, my heart and me.

Now it comes in little darts that fall from all sides at

once. We shield ourselves, and yet one passes by and
hurts us, my heart and me. And the darkness comes and
suffocates us. It is so full of sin. But we emerge again
through his holy name into his holy light, only to be
thrown off again.

It is strange that it should happen on a day when he is
nigh. It isn't that he permitted it. We haven't the sense of
it, my heart and I. Why then is it so that evil comes and
evil goes on soft feet, frightening my heart and me?

Blessed Virgin Mary:
"Because, child, of the free will of men. They can bring
evil wherever they go. Therein lies the mystery of iniquity.
My Son, God, does not will evil at any time. At times, it is
true, he permits in a special way the devil to attack some
souls in order that the same might grow. For each refusal
to commit sin, each fight against temptation, makes man's
will more strong and thus united with my Son's.

"For this he permits the assaults. But free will is free
will. It is a mystery. But slowly you will understand more
of it. Yet mystery it is, like myself and a thousand other
parts of faith.

"You see, you can, and so can they, call up the evil one
by an act of deliberate and free will.

"Of course, it is to be understood that evil, being a
spirit, is everywhere, in a manner of speaking, just waiting for the free will of man to call him in, using from afar
and near all kinds of blandishments to let him in. If one
free will lets him in, it can attack, unless I or my Son stop
it.

"You now are projected into other people's minds, and
you are feeling what they do. It is not your darkness nor
your will. It is an experience of their state. And by enduring it, you received grace. He went to confession, didn't
he? You paid for it by darkness all day.

"You will experience many things in the ascent. Things
are not as they were. But I will be there. Rest in peace."

Lady Pain   *May 19, 1953*

So many thoughts are slashing in my mind. We wander, my heart and I, among these thoughts, and come back to where we started. It all seems most extraordinarily strange.

The road we walk, my heart and I, has no familiar sign at all. It seems we're blindfolded in a way, my heart and I, yet our eyes are wide open.

Then there is pain. Well we know, my heart and I, that we abide in the domain of Lady Pain. But pain from inside, pain from outside, hits us, now at once, now separately, most unexpectedly, encompassing us as if we were in its tight embrace.

We are not used to this as yet, my heart and I. And then we seem to walk the most astounding road, my heart and I. We know it goes up and up, but in truth it is no road at all, barely a path. And what amazes us, my heart and me, is that it is so narrow that we can only walk step by step.

And furthermore, on each side the abysses are bottomless, and we fall. But that isn't all. The road is narrow, steep. The abysses are deep but so narrow; just wide enough for me to fall inside. And on the other side of the abysses lurks darkness and all kinds of shapes; and evil dwells therein personified.

The trees are stunted, and their shapes most horrible. They seem to beget, give birth to, or be the heart of winds so icy cold that my heart and I walk slowly, one foot in front of the other.

Their icy blast numbs us so much that we sort of sway and behold the abysses, the bottomless ones. Well, that is our state these days, my heart and I. But that is not all. Above all this, we really can't quite explain, but we live in a world of light and warmth and delight, my heart and I. We rest, believe it or not, and yet we walk. It puzzles us, my heart and me.

How can it be? Yet we do, in the arms of our love. And we really live in ecstasy, if truth be told. Because from time to time, as men reckon such things, we know the kiss of his mouth, and then we do not care at all about anything.

We are as if we were not, yet we walk. The abysses are there, the stunted trees, the cold. And yet there is ecstasy. And then, incredible as this might seem, we are lifted out of ourselves and led to the rim of time. And then, quite suddenly, time is not, and we are plunged into a sea of love, my heart and I.

It goes like this somehow: God is love, and our Beloved is love made man. And we know without knowing that my heart and I were created to be one with the God-man and that by being one with him, we become one with the Three. And so you see, we walk like that, step by step, and yet at the same time we don't walk at all—we rest.

We are subjected to all this—wind, abyss, and dark, and yet we live in light. We are in time and yet we are outside of it.

You see why it is so strange for us, my heart and me. And we don't know if we are alive or dead or why or how. For in us, somehow, time and eternity meet. Well, they say there is death in between. But we are alive. Or are we dead? We don't know, my heart and I. That is why we want some help, my heart and I.

Pentecost   *May 21, 1953*

The Holy Spirit descends into this room.

"I am the Spirit of Love, the Crimson Dove, the flame of Love. I am the giver of all gifts divine, and I perfect the work of love in the souls of men. I am the Love between the Father and the Son, Creator blest. I come but rarely. This time I came to strengthen the faith, that it might be strong and straight; to uphold trust that is complete and make it deep; to take into myself abandonment that has been growing—fruit divine, in this soul of predilection that is mine.

"Oh, it began so long ago on a tall hill, when I descended into this soul and blessed the seeds, already planted there before, of these three that were to be the foundation of this life of grace. The others were there, of course, but these three belong to her especially. They are the virtues of the land she comes from, and few understand because of that. My spouse, Mary, loves these with tender love. That is why she loves this child of predilection whom she calls her own.

"This is my time, Lover divine. I descend with a special intensity now. For that is the way I came, a wind, a mighty wind, that on that day became visible to men. Listen. Hear the wind today. I roam at will, but then I stop on my way. My flaming tips touch this soul or that, and then their ascent is faster towards us, the Three that are One. I stop today because faith is great, and the soul abandoned, going toward charity, rooted in humility and obedience. Of such is the light that pierces the darkness of the earth and lifts men up to me.

"She has been a clear channel of that grace, and endless, it would seem to you, if you could see what she brought to me. She won't know I passed this way. She won't know the wind kissed her face. She won't know the flaming tips of my wings touched her heart and made it stronger in faith and trust. This is the time I descended on the earth in my fecundity of love. There is the wind of it. There is myself."

God's Light   *September 1953*

My heart and I were locked in a deep night, alone, afraid and sad beyond all sadness. There was about us much fear, and we felt lost and fell onto the bitter dust of the unknown road we had stood on in the dark night.

And then, quite suddenly, we saw a light, and someone with a heart full of light was bending over our nothingness and emptiness and lifting us, so full of heaviness and dust, into a place of warmth and rest.

My heart and I were weak and blind and did not see or know the light that came and made away with our dark night and had the strength to lift the heavy dead weight of us into a place of rest.

But then, when we awoke again, we knew that it was the light of the house of God that drew the bleak curtains of our night away and that we rested in its heart that day.

My Lover Came   *October 4, 1955*

My Lover came into my fearsome night, so bleak, so dark, and made it bright with his divine and burning light. He bent so low and lifted me into the very heart of ecstasy! And then, he held me at arms length and bade me look and see the gifts he had given me. When lost in deserts and in nights so dark, so filled with pain, I was like one without sight, quite blind.

Now, in his light that was so warm and bright, I saw myself bedecked in red, the color of his precious Blood. I saw a crown of rubies upon my head, where thorns had brought a maddening pain into my night!

I saw some precious stones adorn my naked feet. They glowed more red than the rubies did upon my head. I saw my hands laden with bands and rings, all red and precious stones that shone like fire in the night.

He spoke again, so soft, so low. I had to bend my soul to catch the whispers of his loving voice: "Behold my gifts to you, my love. Wilt thou give me just one gift back for all of these? Lift up thy earthly love. Give me back the one* I gave thee, the one who sings such songs to her

who gave me flesh. Lift up and give me back her troubadour she loves so much.

"But you must give your earthly love to me most joy-
ously and freely, as freely as a bird gives songs to the
rising and descending sun."

In silent answer, I took my earthly love, the troubadour
of Mary's songs, and, with a strength I never had before, I
lifted him high, high, up, up above, and saw the pierced
hands of my mystic Love receive my earthly one. And
then I saw the Mother of all priests vest him in vestments
white and blinding bright. Then take him by the hand
and lead him to an altar filled with light, and bid him to
offer her Son in sacrifice.

*Her husband, Eddie Doherty.

Weep Not, Beloved   *December 7, 1956*

My heart is lifted to the Lord, imploring, begging, cry-
ing for that gift of fire which is love.

My heart is all desire to burn with the love of God, so
that a thousand sparks of such a fire may fall and kindle
other hearts.

My heart is hunger, thirst, waiting to be filled with
God. It is a chalice, waiting, waiting to be so filled with
love that it may spill this love upon the earth. I tremble
with desire to set on fire the world for God.

Behold my poverty. I do not wonder that God will
come; for he is love and my need of loving will direct him
close.

My heart is ready to be enlarged, wounded by a sword
and lance of pain. Oh Love, do not delay, and let this
heart serve as a trough for your immense and everlasting
love.

Let it become a table to fit right within the stable of Bethlehem. Let all who hunger eat from it. For I have eaten you, and so I am ready to be all eaten up for you. Oh Jesus, come, delay not. The waiting is torture excruciating. Yet this too I lift to you.

Weep not, Beloved. Behold the misery of men. See, I am unfolding my soul, a cloth to wipe your tears. I know their weight will prostrate me flat upon the earth. But my very lying upon its dust will stop a passer-by. That passing of his will bring your Mother nigh, and all will be well then.

Your wounds beholding, I offer the wine of my life to moisten your lips so parched and dried. See. Hear. I opened my heart with your lance of love and out of its very substance I saved healing unguents. Weak, poor, unworthy, I will find strength to lift your wounded body and bring it to the inn of my loving heart.

I will not leave you to the mercy of strangers, innkeepers, and such, but spend myself, my days, my nights, in long and loving watch.

And if your pains linger, I'll kneel and beg from you the grace, the strength, to carry your pain for you.

Yes!   *February 24, 1957*

He asked me once, long, long ago, if I would love him as he loved me. Young, gay, joyous, I answered, "Yes, indeed!" And then he smiled, and instead of a wedding ring, he gave me his pain.

Since then, I have not slept. My soul refused all rest. It was on fire with one desire—to heal his pain.

I have become an outcast of love and fire. My desire urges me on. That is why you see my heart, a wanderer, a fiery dart, that goes right up into his heart, and falls right down back on the earth to shed his fire.

I wonder as I wander: where shall I find oils and balms to heal his pain? True, I am a beggar; but I know that gold and silver will not buy love's healing.

I know that I must pierce my heart and die of love, for drop by drop my blood will mingle with his. The mingling will be the only balm he will take to heal his wounds.

Abyss   *Lent, 1958*

Into an abyss dark, I know I must enter now and face the smell of death and loneliness laced with the light of hope.

I know that I must face again a searing pain. I know that fear will make me cringe and then stand up and fall again in endless mental pain.

I know that darkness stands and waits to cover me, and I feel a joy, a pain, a fear come nearer and nearer.

I want to be as swift as wind to meet them all. And I want to run and hide away from them.

School of Saints   *April 8, 1958*

"To take, to leave, to permit, to throw, to permit darkness and distress, to caress, to allow the foe to buffet, to tear, to wound and disturb.

"Then to present dancing stars, and permit the Mother of Grace to appear; then cloud the sky, plaything of my love. How did you like my gift of yesterday? A star at your feet!

"You were startled and flew like a dove, and ran like a doe. But you received the star and the flame of my love. That is the way. And right after that, with my star still reflected in your eyes, I permitted the foe to attack so that you might heal. For my gifts I do not take back.

"But remember, that is the way of it, up and down, to be left to hang on a tree alone, to be lifted up in splendid garments. For, bride of my soul, you too began like I. You had no place to lay your head. You fled, too, to Egypt land, and then hiddenly, humbly, laboriously, from laundry to factory, from Greek to Greek, you lived the way of Nazareth. And now you enter the public life.

"But since man's time is limited, and though I renew your youth like the eagle's, parallel is your public life to my passion. That is why you find my ways strange. The ways will be harder still, and stranger, before I call you into my Heart to enjoy its joys forever. Prepare yourself now to live as I want you to live. For this is the time you train in the school of saints, my dear."

Chapels   *Lent, 1958*

The little chapels, and the small, forgotten wayside shrines, as well as huge and awesome churches, you seek to make me thine!

Grey, nondescript, sad creatures. Tremendous Lover, Lord of all Hosts, do you behold the utter me as I am? Or does your love extend to such as I, who knows but one thing: I am.

Macabre Dance   *March, 1959*

Dance your macabre dance. Twist, hurl, whirl my soul into your cold and bleak domain. Let the refrain of your hate ambulate all that I am.

Twirl, whirl, hurl my soul about your hell. Set the knell of your carillon through my hair like the wild sound of death.

See, I am pliant and go to and fro with the hurricane dance of your hate, early or late. Yet I am with light.

Your music of hell, your fiendish delight in my plight, have not extinguished the light.

Beyond Knowing   *October 31, 1959*

There is a knowing beyond unknowing. I have been there, and learned but one thing—that I am *nothing,* and He is *all.*

There is a fire that consumes without consuming. I stood within it, and learned but one thing—that nothingness can burn like that!

There is a hunger that is a pain beyond enduring. I endured that, and learned that nothingness can hunger too.

There is a sweetness that flows like nectar, in endless streams of joy intense, like the caress of a Lover who is content. I know this sweetness, it comes to me now and then. I know that nothingness can faint with love and joy.

There is an ecstasy so strange, so high, so intense, that just to touch its rim is to not be. I know, it touched and annihilated me. And then I knew that nothingness is true, but that He who is knowing in unknowing, Fire, Hunger, Joy, Desire, can, with a touch, make nothingness into *himself.*

To A Poor Clare   *Christmas, 1959*

A Child is born to us. Oh wonder! He is God.

Behold love lies so small, a manger can hold it all.

Yet beholding his smallness, immensity is suddenly encompassed by glance and touch.

No wonder the wonder of the Child, the crib, the stable holds our hearts.

UNDATED ENTRIES

Who Am I?

Today my heart and I remember so many things that seemed to have got lost along the way of our journey. They come, they go, like fleeting clouds on a clear summer day.

Who am I today that I should stay on earth and make believe that I am the "I" who was so long ago? For I am not the "I" who lived so many years in a strange world of men and deeds, of life and death and pain and tears.

Today I am a flame, a light, that burns bright and consumes me all without consuming. I am a hunger that knows it cannot eat its fill. I am a wanderer who has no home. For how can I rest in my quest for love that I must touch now and again or die a thousand deaths?

What am I today but emptiness that must be filled. I walk on earth and dream of heaven. I am as restless as the

seas and yet as still as a mighty tree. I am all light, yet
often I live in utter darkness, lightless and bleak. I am a
contradiction to myself.

Today my heart and I remember so many things that
seemed to have got lost along the way of our journey.

Days of Joy, Days of Pain

My heart and I are gay today, dancing away into the
blue of Our Lady's day. And yet my heart and I know that
for us the blue is edged with black.

My heart and I are full of joy today, and songs all clear
as flutes and reeds that reach as far as the stars of Our
Lady's crown. And yet my heart and I know watchfulness
that speaks of silence and of tears.

My heart and I splash and swim and then lie still, content with the thousand tendernesses of Our Lady's clear
white day, so warm, so fresh, so gay. And yet we know,
my heart and I, that cold winds wait by the gate and will
blow away our gay day and leave us shivering and cold.

Slowly the lovely day goes all away in the strange gray
of the time between night and day called twilight. And
my heart and I watch it go and know that now the echo of
its footsteps sing a Miserere. We do not mind the coming
or the going of any day. We take each one, and then we
give it back all filled with love to her who gives it to her
Son.

My heart and I know full well that there will be days of
dark and pain, and days of silence and of grief, too deep
for tears. And then days so filled with tears that they will
make a river, bittersweet, to wash the filth away of many
in that day. And then again there will be days so gay that
we will laugh and dance and sing and be glad so as to be
ready to be sad again.

My heart and I are ready for all days our Love sends to us. For they are all but ladders, stepping stones, to the one when finally he and we shall be one.

Quest

My heart is a stranger today. It has left me and gone, wandered off and away. Am I heart-less? Oh no. He gave me his heart when mine wandered away.

My heart is a stranger today. But where has it gone? Has it really wandered away? Or has it made its way into the place where his heart used to be before he gave his to me?

My heart is a stranger today. And yet maybe I gave it away yesterday, when I knew that he wanted a gift, and I so poor had nothing to give but my heart.

Was it then that he sent that strange sleep that was not a sleep at all but more like a strange state of being and not being at all? It was then that I felt the pain that would have made me cry out if I had had a voice to voice a cry. But I was and I was not, and as such I was voiceless as one dead yet living.

Was there a moment that pierced like a knife when he bent and accepted the gift of my heart? Was there sleep or death or the essence of life when he gave me his heart in exchange?

I am woundless, and yet I know without knowing that I have a wounded heart that lives but to give and to weep that its giving is often in vain.

I am tearless. And yet my heart is a fountain of tears that keeps flowing with infinite tenderness that seeks but to heal and make whole.

I am flameless for all to see. And yet I know without knowing that my heart that consumes me without consuming lights all it can touch with a flame that partakes of the searing flame of the second Person of the Trinity.

He took my heart and gave me his. And now my fearful heart has lost its fear, and I have a wounded heart that is a flame that burns without rest on its eternal quest for souls.

Desire

My heart and I are quiet today, and still, with the stillness of gentle rain, of a wood standing still in its white, bright mantle of snow. Still like a bird all asleep in its nest, at rest. Still as the ocean is some days when all alone in the night, it chants the praise of God with its utter might. Still as the night waiting in utter recollection for the dawn to come and give her sleep.

My heart and I are quiet today and still under the gentle touch of pain. The quiet deepens, and we are still as if we were not there but somewhere else—we know not where.

My heart and I are quiet today and oh, so still. Yet we are a candle white that burns bright with an unearthly fire, a strange desire. The quiet is quieter, the stillness deeper, and our desire is there.

My heart and I are cut apart and one of us is free to start and meet desire. We do not know who stays behind, my heart or I, to burn brighter and light the path that goes so straight upward. But one of us takes flight and needs no light, for upward is desire, and desire is so bright, it is all light. Yet within that light there is a fire where one of us will meet desire and be consumed utterly, eternally.

Only not yet, not now. Because, behold, we are again together, my heart and I, still and quiet as ever, and yet full of desire.

Treasure Hunters

My heart and I are treasure hunters. We cannot rest. We cannot sleep. My heart and I are treasure hunters, treasure hunters of the deep.

Into the depths we dive and search for treasures old and treasures new. Into the heights we fly to gather stardust where we may, my heart and I.

Into the fields, into the dales, we wander, restless like a flame, in search of rubies, emeralds and any precious stones my heart and I, treasure hunters, can find. Unto the peaks, dark and bleak, my heart and I climb unafraid in search of all unknown things that will make treasures for a heart divine.

But we are sad, my heart and I, of treasures new or old. The heights elude us; we cannot catch the stars, and stardust passes us by, my heart and I.

The fields and dales are empty wastes. They have no greens, no reds; the blues are gone. No precious stones are left to us to find. Oh restless heart, oh tired mind. The peaks are dark and oh so bleak, and yield not even one unknown thing of beauty to adorn God's loving heart.

And so my restless heart and I are empty-handed and alone. Lost treasure hunters of depths and heights.

Stand still, oh restless heart. For you are now my only gift to his so deeply wounded heart. Stand still, oh restless heart, and try to see what treasures may be hidden in thee. Stand still, oh restless heart. Die within me so that I may lay thee in his wounds, a flame of ecstasy.

Nazareth

My heart and I were in Palestine tonight. Strange, holy was our flight. We went somehow back in time. In an instant we flew along the road of centuries which ceased abruptly at Nazareth.

It was the hour of twilight. The world seemed hushed in a strange expectancy of hope. We touched the hem of it, trembling with the joy of it.

The house we entered was small, the chamber smaller still. A girl-child, yet a woman, sat still, and with motions so few spun white threads that seemed to be all melody.

We did not know, my heart and I, why we trembled so, nor why we wished to veil our face. All we knew is that we were and were not, and all in us was light, silence deep, that worshiped like a flame at a shrine we could not as yet see.

Divine Outcast And I

My heart and I are breathless tonight, breathless with stardust that blinds our eyes and makes us lose all sense of time and space and throws us into specks of dust, into infinity.

My heart and I are breathless tonight with holy joy that makes stars out of stardust for us to climb infinity and span time.

My heart and I are breathless tonight for we are dancing, dancing to the music of love tonight. It came to us in a baby's cry, a woman's eyes, a man's sob, a priest's word, and the song of youth.

My heart and I are breathless tonight, with stardust in our eyes, with holy joy, with love divine.

My heart and I are still tonight, in a strange breathless way. It seems as if my heart and I are all aflame tonight with love. A love that started like a spark and now is an all consuming flame that is immense, intense and growing, growing still, in height, in depth, in width.

Oh breathless heart that stands so still, will you and I

burn so much that we become consumed, absorbed in him who came back from the tomb? Alleluia!

Stillness and Motion

In utter stillness, void and light, my heart and I abide today. And yet there is about the stillness a motion of such force that though it moves in endless creative love, it moves so fast that it stands still to us.

In the motion that is as if it were all stillness, we were drawn in by a light that shone against a night that was all bleak and dark, as darkness was before love bade light to be.

The light that drew us into itself and out of ourselves was light itself. And then we knew, my heart and I, without knowing, what love looks like, that it is all light of loving.

In essence and in truth we stood, my heart and I, alone; and yet without knowing, we knew that we were one with both, for both were light, and light was love, and love was God.

It was and is as if we crossed somehow, somewhere, the great divide that in itself has no being, yet is called time and timelessness.

With us walks hunger, immense and burning, that will consume us without consuming, until some day we will go away into the moving stillness, the light that is uncreated Love, not to return. We know now, my heart and I, how one can burn from hungering for the light that is all delight, and for which there is no filling this side of the divide.

We know, my heart and I, that it is that burning that fills us with a searing, endless pain of joy that gives the light that comes from us, a light we must not hide but show in utter perfect charity that feeds on pain that makes

us grow and thus become a bigger light to light the falter-
ing feet of men to God.

Love is like that. It dies a thousand deaths for its beloved, and finds a thousand lives to live again from each
of its dyings.

My heart and I are ready now for any dying, for only
then can we go on loving. And so, oh uncreated Light
that is all light, my Lord and God, show us the way to
constant, utter dying, for timelessness holds time within
its breast and both are one.

But we somehow, somewhere, crossed the non-
existing, immense divide between time and timelessness,
and were absorbed, encompassed, taken in by a stillness
that is all motion and light, that is light uncreated, that
always was and is and shall be in all eternity.

That is the Word. We dwelt in it. In time we walked
outside of space and yet were held by it. We were not
dead, and yet we were as dead. And in that deathless
death we knew eternal life that stemmed from life.

And now we are back into space and time, ourselves a
light, and yet not our own, but lighted from the Light that
drew us in so suddenly from the dark night and then sent
us, a light, back into the night.

That is why in utter stillness, void and light, my heart
and I abide today and wait and wait to go away again into
the light that is all love, that is our God; when the Light
will draw us nigh again to him.

My Heart Has Left Its Moorings

My heart has left its moorings. It seems so free to float
and see the world.

My heart has left its moorings. But it closed its eyes.

I ask you, friend, who wants to see our world today?—
God alone does.

Song Of Tears

A strange, tear-shaped transparency, envelops me. It seems that my heart and I are in an ocean of salty tears that is composed of an infinity of one by one; and each is slowly trickling into my heart, and soon my heart and I will drown in them.

Each tear bears within its translucency a face, and each face is the same, full of pain, with tears shed or unshed lying beneath its bones; an ocean of tears that all belong to men and are all contained in the strange transparency that envelops me and is one tear of Christ.

The ocean of tears that are one, and yet come at my heart and me one by one, has a song that haunts me now and pierces my heart with swords so sharp that it seems that very soon my heart may die, or start to take the song of tears unto itself.

My Retreat

Our Lady of the hand, please take my hand in thine, and lead me to the sanctuary, the house of bread, where my retreat is to be made.

Look at her long, and see the perfect modesty and grace of person in her face. With eyes cast down and hands half hidden in her veil, she speaks to me of what my attitude must be. She talks to none but in whose charge she is, nor thinks of aught but Jesus in her heart.

She touches lightly all that she must use, nor clings to any one. They are indeed gifts of God's love, and speak to her of him. From that first moment when he came as man, they form a part of him, and thus they are entitled to respect, but can be loved and used only in him. Yet in very truth she hardly heeds them, for her heart cleaves to the God who made them; so they become part of the worship which she pays to him.

And what of that, the worship of her God? What reverent simplicity is hers, what faith, hope, love. Who can describe it? The virtues and the gifts that make her full of grace, God has bestowed on her first for her Son and then for us. Mediatrix of all graces is her title now. And she is generous as is mother love. So ask her and you will not be denied.

Sweet Lady, hear our prayer and grant us grace to make a good retreat.

She Is The Gate

My heart and I went to school today. An angel showed us the way. Through clouds of gray that were all blue and lined with strange and unknown hues, he took us up and up and up, and brought us to a gate.

It was a strange and wondrous gate of wood that seemed to come from trees unknown on earth. They had a sheen, a tinge of red, that shone from within like a golden thread.

The wood was plain. There were no intricate designs. Just two upright planed and polished trees with a bar across. And yet, because of the light without and within, the logs, the gate appeared as if they were wrought in marvelous designs that all the men on earth had ever wrought. And then it seemed the triune God put the finishing touches on it.

We stood entranced before the sight of it, my heart and I, and of the tender green grass flecked with flowers of the fields the gate stood in. But it was time to enter through the gate and walk across the tender grass flecked with the blending shades of every field flower ever made.

It was time to enter our school of love that would teach us the ways of knowing, serving, loving our Love, and the short cuts of finding him for whom our heart died so constantly of a thousand fiery desires.

And so we walked through the strange gate and passed across the tender fields of green. And there we were before a Woman who stood stock still. She did not even look to see my heart and me enter inside her empty, tidy room.

We did not know, my heart and I, what we had to do. And yet, in utter simplicity we sat on the plain wooden floor at her hidden feet.

Time ceased to be. Her silence entered into us and filled us to the brim. Then it began to fill every part of us. We felt as if its mantle light fell on us like a blinding sight. We thought it entered the very essence of us, my heart and me. It seemed as if it were a knife so sharp that with a swoop it cut us off all things of earth and brought us into its domain for good.

Then suddenly it changed and became a warm sea and we, my heart and I, a drop in it. Then we understood quite simply how one can be and yet not be, for we were lost within that sea, and yet we knew our own ecstasy.

The waves of the sea of silence that encompassed my heart and me brought us quite gently on the shores of all silence, on the shores of love who is God. For love speaks without words, and so this silence begets all beauty of sounds that creation knows.

We lay on the shore—or was it his heart?—and we knew the secret of love. We knew that the key to the shore and the sea was a Woman who lived, spoke, and walked this earth, and yet never left the heart of her God who used her to bring his silence on earth.

Strange, but it seems that my heart and I have brought from her today some of that silence with us. It seems as if it were given to us to share with those who come to her house of love.

For it seems that she has decided now to bring them all to her school of love, and that Lesson One is silence of heart under pain, joy, and darkness.

Yes, my heart and I went to school today.

Mary's Atonement

My heart and I are sad tonight, with the strange heavy sadness of all yesterdays and all todays, and even all tomorrows not born yet. The sadness grows and we look on, my heart and I, and know that now it will fall on us and crush us under its weight. And that is why my heart and I are so terribly afraid tonight.

My heart and I are in the dark tonight, a dark so strange that we know we never saw the like of it before. It is the dark of Mary's tears that lie unshed in her heart, all filled with seven swords that cut and pierce but do not kill her Mother's heart.

But the darkness of her one tear may kill us, my heart and me. For it is made of love that men have thrown away; and it was filled with many gifts for them to have. And now behold, they all are there in the dust of a thousand roads, and men walk and crush her gifts with their dirty feet. And I weep as does my heart in the strange darkness of Mary's tear.

And then on us, my heart and me, descends a cloud that crucifies us in its utter agony of fear. For we are here tonight, my heart and I, to stop that cloud and lift it up.

But oh, the fear that fills us full before the cloud of God's Fatherhood, descending on the land of men who trample on one of Mary's tears.

And then tonight we must take on a sadness that is our own; the sadness that our land is filled to overflowing, like the chalice of the Lord.

Oh heart of mine, make ready then to drink the sadness to its last drop.

My Heart Is A Dancer

My heart is a dancer. It dances away its life, sad or gay. It dances in shadows, it dances in light, but always it dances its life away.

My heart is a dancer now abandoned and gay, now lost in a mad whirl of grief or hope, but always dancing its life away.

My heart is a dancer to music that men do not know. It follows the song of the wind in the leaves wherever it goes. But always it dances its life away.

My heart is a dancer to the song of flames and the music of snow and of rain. But always it dances its life away.

My heart is a dancer that weaves a design of love and desires that take birth in pain, but always it dances its life away.

My heart is a dancer of passion that spans time and eternity. But always it dances its life away.

My heart is a dancer, graceful and light like the beam of the sun or the darkness of night. But always it dances its life away.

My heart is a dancer, for then it can sing its hymn to the lover that is not there. But always it dances its life away.

Dance, my heart. Dance and sing. For only in death will you know him to whose music you sing.

Alphabetical Index

OTHER TITLES FROM ST. BEDE'S

The Steps of Love
In *The Dialogue* of St. Catherine of Siena
Mary Ann Follmar (Dominican)
The Dialogue of St. Catherine of Siena usually meets with a bewildered response from readers. As an aid to discovering the richness of this mystical treatise, the author introduces the spiritual journey outlined in *The Dialogue* and comments on the insights provided therein toward spiritual growth.
Paperback, 84 pages $4.95   ISBN 0-932506-17-8

Lamps of Fire: Studies in Christian Mysticism
Robert Herrera
Pseudo-Denis, Bonaventure, Ramon Lull, and Teresa of Avila—their mystical teachings studied in the context of their lives, historical circumstances, and influence on future Christian mystical writers. A beautiful book of readings!
Paperback, 138 pages $7.95   ISBN 0-932506-40-2

A Touch of God: Eight Monastic Journeys
edited by Maria Boulding, OSB
Eight monks and nuns share with you their intimate thoughts and personal experiences in discovering faith in God, and show that through the insecurities of life, with its failures and mistakes, there runs a thread of blessedness. A captivating book that will help you to recognize the touch of God in your own life.
Paperback, 180 pages $7.95   ISBN 0-932506-26-7

The Glory of Thy People
Raphael Simon, OCSO
The spiritual odyssey of a Jewish psychiatrist, a convert to the Catholic faith, who left a promising career to become a monk in one of the strictest Orders of the Church. To Dr. Simon, the Catholic faith was the natural continuation of the Jewish faith: not a cleavage, but an evolvement. A fascinating book!
Paperback, 133 pages $6.95   ISBN 0-932506-47-X

A Padre Pio Profile

John A. Schug, OFM, Cap

Interviews with several of Padre Pio's confreres in the friary at San Giovanni Rotondo, and with some of his spiritual children who received cures or special graces through his prayers. New or little-known information is brought out in these interviews concerning the Padre's fruitful spiritual life. The book ends with an up-to-date account of the canonization process being conducted for Padre Pio's cause.

Paperback, 163 pages $6.95   **ISBN 0-932506-56-9**

The Last of the Fathers

M. Basil Pennington, OCSO

In this book, which is written with brilliance and fine sensitivity, learn how St. Bernard and his followers radically changed monasticism and the Church itself. While reading, you will feel the force and charm of Bernard's personality and the other great Cistercian Fathers.

Paperback, 297 pages $14.95   **ISBN 0-932506-24-0**

A Guide to Monastic Communities
in the Northeast

This guide is a valuable source for those who are searching or for those who are just curious about the monastic life. Twenty-three communities in the Northeastern United States describe themselves and their lifestyles in individual articles with photographs.

Paperback, 46 pages $2.00

The Benedictine Way

Wulstan Mork, OSB

Written as a commentary on the vows for monks and nuns, this little book is meant for all of us who are hungering for deeper prayer. Benedictine prayer is simple and direct, and this guide will take you back to the sources of Christian spirituality. This gem is destined to be a spiritual classic!

Paperback, 95 pages $5.95   **ISBN 0-932506-32-1**

I Believe in Love
Father Jean D'Elbee, SS.CC.
Treat yourself to a mini-retreat with this jewel of a book filled with spiritual nourishment. The book consists of retreat conferences given by the author based on the spirituality of St. Therese of Lisieux.
Paperback, 157 pages $4.95   **ISBN 0-932506-25-9**

Spirituality Recharted
Hubert van Zeller, OSB
In this delightful book, Dom Hubert discusses the pursuit of sanctity "by responding to the grace of spirituality," as he puts into everyday language St. John of the Cross' treatment of the soul's progress toward union with God. A best-seller!
Paperback, 157 pages $4.95   **ISBN 0-932506-39-9**

Reflections
Charles Rich
In this profound book Charles Rich will help you in your search for personal growth in holiness. Each short chapter is full of spiritual wisdom and covers such topics as the mystery of our own being, love without limits, and the nature of prayer.
Paperback, 131 pages $6.95   **ISBN 0-932506-49-6**

Victory Over Death
Ronda Chervin
This beautiful book is meant for all of us, to show us that nothing in the world can compare with the joys of heaven. It will help you to deal with all aspects of death—your own or that of a loved one—and offers suggestions for developing your own preparation for *Victory over Death*. A great gift book!
Paperback, 63 pages $3.95   **ISBN 0-932506-43-7**

Gateway to Hope
Maria Boulding, OSB
"Learning to deal with failure is a part of life," says the author, a contemplative nun of Stanbrook Abbey, England. In this latest book, Sister Maria draws on human experience and on the Bible to show that in our very failure lies our success.
Paperback, 158 pages $5.95   Not Available in Canada

The Liturgy of the Hours
Dominic Scotto, TOR
The Liturgy of the Hours has generally been thought of as the exclusive prerogative of clergy and religious. The liturgical reform of Vatican II directed that it be once again restored to its original purpose as a prayer for the entire People of God. Fr. Scotto presents a historical overview of the development of the Divine Office and helps you understand the significance this prayer of the Church should have in your life. Included are practical guidelines for implementing the Divine Office on the parish level.
Paperback, 213 pages $9.95   ISBN 0-932506-48-8

There Shines Forth Christ
Dom Julian Stead, OSB
This exquisite volume of poetry will elicit an enthusiastic response, as the author shares his own feelings for God, man, and nature. *"The finest Christian poetry in English of our times...pure prayer, deep and holy."* **From the Introduction by Sheldon Vanauken**
Paperback, 156 pages $8.95   ISBN 0-932506-29-1

Order From:

St. Bede's Publications
P.O. Box 545
Petersham, MA 01366-0545 USA
(617) 724-3407

Please allow 4 weeks for delivery
Prices subject to change without notice
Send for our complete catalog of books and tapes